USN AIRCRAFT CARRIER AIR UNITS

Volume 2
1957-1963

by DUANE A KASULKA

Illustrated by Don Greer

squadron/signal publications

DEDICATED:

To my oldest son, Duane A Kasulka II who aspires to become a Naval Officer

ACKNOWLEDGEMENTS

The author wishes to thank the following individuals and organizations for their assistance in providing photographic and research material. A special mention regarding the extra effort contributed by the following five individuals.

Mike Grove   Bill Larkins   Larry Smalley   Bill Swisher   Clay Jansson
Thank you very much

Jack Anderson	Jeff Fister	Lional Paul
Al Bachmann	Harry Gann	Fred Roos
Roger Besecker	Fred Harl	Jim Sullivan
Warren Bodie	Frank Hartman	Gren Rich
Peter Bowers	Larry Kasulka	Bruce Trombecky
Bob Carlisle	Toda Koda	Gordon Williams
Bob Esposito	Bob Lawson	Nick Williams
John Elliot	Lois Lovisolo	
Tail Hook	Gerry Margraff	McDonnell Douglas
North American	Grumman Aerospace	
		United States Navy
Naval Aviation News	Vought Corp	
	United States	
	Marine Corps	

(Above) F4D-1 Skyrays (139165 and 134884) of VF-141 poised to launch from RANGER (CVA-61) during the carrier's first cruise in 1959. On their return VF-141 transitioned to the F3H Demon. (MDAC via Harry Gann)

(Below) A-4C (A4D-2N) Skyhawks of VA-34 heading back to SARATOGA (CVA-60) during 1963. Their colorful Blue trim colors are typical of those being used by Fleet Squadrons. (USN)

(Above) F8U-1P (145629) Crusader of VFP-62, DET-65 launches while an F4H-1 (151428) of VF-102 awaits its turn. This was the ENTERPRISE's (CVAN-65) first cruise and it returned from the Med in time to support the Cuban Quarantine during October of 1962. (USN)

USN AIRCRAFT CARRIER AIR UNITS 1957-1963

By mid 1950 the United States Navy was faced with an increasingly uneasy international cold war and the possibility of a nuclear war. The Korean War had demonstrated the importance of conventional weapons, but US military policy was centered around the thesis that there would be no major conflict without the use of nuclear weapons. The US Navy achieved true strategic capability with the arrival of the first of the new super carriers, USS FORRESTAL (CVA-59) in 1955. This was the first post war built carrier and had the capability of operating nuclear armed jet aircraft. Four sister ships were authorized at the rate of approximately one per year. Navy plans were to eventually have twelve of these new FORRESTAL class carriers with the possibility of nuclear propulsion on later versions. Along with the three MIDWAY class carriers, the Fleet would have fifteen attack carriers.

In 1956 the French and British and Israelis carried out a military intervention in Egypt in order to keep the Suez Canal open. The Cold War had been heated up by the Soviet-bloc with near flood level arms shipments into the Middle East to further their repeatedly stated objective of global conquest. There had been an aborted military coup in Jordan that was inspired by the newly formed United Arab Republic (UAR) made up of Egypt and Syria. The Sixth Fleet was called in for a show of force during April to discourage the UAR from armed intervention in Jordan. Armed rebellion followed in Lebanon in May. In July a bloody coup in Iraq killed the pro-western king. Lebanon, fearing a communist inspired revolution requested US help on the 15th of May. The only available force was portions of the Sixth Fleet which sent Marines ashore the next day with eleven aircraft as air cover! In just over a week 350 aircraft aboard five US carriers were available and by October the situation had stabilized and US forces were withdrawn.

On 25 August 1958 the Nationalist Chinese off shore Islands of Quemoy came under an artillery attack from Communist China. This time the Seventh Fleet was placed on alert and ordered to prepare for major operations against Communist China. Additional carriers were called in to patrol the Formosa Straits and escort Nationalist Chinese supply ships to an from the islands being shelled. The Fleet buildup plus that of USAF and USMC convinced the Communists that the US commitment was real and the shelling was quickly reduced.

August of 1960 saw the missile rattling of Russia's Premier Khrushchev in response to the United State's and United Nation's intervention in the Congo strife. Again the Fleet was called on to move forces into both the Mediterranean and the Pacific. Three CVAs were provided in both locations. To maintain six aircraft carriers continually on station required eighteen, but the Navy was able to briefly scrape together only sixteen carriers with the arrival of the KITTYHAWK (CVA-63) in April 1961, the CONSTELLATION (CVA-64) in October, the nuclear powered ENTERPRISE (CVAN-65) in November, and by retaining older ESSEX carriers.

(Above) F8U-1 (145466) Crusader of VF-154 being waved off CORAL SEA (CVA-43) in March of 1961. The compactness of a carrier deck can be seen by the mix of A3D Skywarriors (VAH-2), AD Skyraiders (VA-152), and A4D Skyhawks (VA-153 and VA-155) tied down along the edge of the deck. (USN)

(Below) F-3B (F3H-2) (143492) Demon of VF-13 Aggressors being hoisted aboard SHANGRI LA (CVA-38) in October of 1963 prior to departing Mayport. This is the normal method for loading aircraft aboard a carrier for a deployment. (USN)

(Below) A4D-2 (145061) Skyhawk of VMA-324 in CAG-7 markings. VMA-324 and VMA-121 A4D-2s based at NAF Asugi, Japan replaced the fighter squadrons VF-151 and VF-154 while CORAL SEA (CVA-43) operated in the Western Pacific. The objective was to evaluate an all attack group during the CORAL SEA's 1960/61 cruise. (USN)

3

(Above) F3H-2 Demons of VF-31 Felix attached to CVG-3 on SARATOGA (CVA-60) in 1962 during the carrier's fourth cruise (all to the Med). The F3H was the Navy's first all-weather fighter. (USN)

Events in the Caribbean in April of 1961 forced the Navy to station carriers off the coast of Cuba during the Bay of Pigs invasion. The Sixth Fleet was back again in June when the Dominican Republic's dictator Trujillo was assassinated and an uprising seemed imminent. In November the Sixth Fleet was patrolling off the coast of Guatemala and Nicaragua when their governments requested US assistance to prevent communist led invasions of their nations.

(Below) AD-6 (137546) Skyraider of VA-104 Hell's Archers refueling an F8U-1P (144613) Crusader of VFP-62, DET-42 in August of 1958 as part of CVG-10 off FORRESTAL (CVA-59), during the carrier's first cruise. Aerial refueling was adopted for all Navy aircraft in 1958. (MDAC)

Next followed Soviet pressure on Berlin which began with the erection of the Berlin Wall in 1961. The US responded by increasing the readiness of its armed forces. For the Navy this included the addition of an attack carrier air group, and an ASW carrier air group. Increased tension followed, and in October thirteen Naval Reserve squadrons were activated. They were released the following year in August. Next followed a cease fire violation by the communist forces in Laos in May of 1962. The 7th Fleet was ordered to support neighboring Thailand and back up US diplomatic efforts to save the independence of Laos.

In October of 1962 President Kennedy revealed the presence of Soviet missiles in Cuba and he responded by ordering a naval and air quarantine of the Island. Low-level photographic reconnaissance aircraft had revealed the missile pressence. A total of eight carriers took part in the quarantine before it was declared ended with the removal of the Soviet missiles in November.

In the following pages this seven year period (1957 to 1963) of increased world tension, the aircraft types, force levels, the markings, and the color schemes employed by carrier air units will be discussed.

CARRIERS

In the early 1950s US attack carriers (CVAs) were WWII ESSEX Class carriers, of which fifteen had been modernized for jet operations from 1948 through 1955. The major modifications to accommodate the heavier fuel hungry jets was a strengthened and angled flight deck, increased fuel capability, steam catapults, more powerful arresting gear, and removal of the twin 5-inch gun mounts to add deck space. The remaining straight deck ESSEX carriers and a few light carriers (CVLs) were designated Anti-Submarine Warfare (ASW) carriers (CVSs). MIDWAY class carriers were also modernized with the same features as the ESSEX class carriers plus the addition of a third catapult.

FORRESTAL class super-carriers were considerably larger than MIDWAY class carriers since they had been built especially to handle the larger jets and carry out all weather operations. By 1958 fifteen CVAs were operational; three FORRESTAL, two MIDWAY, and ten ESSEX class. It was late 1958 before the Western Pacific saw its first super carrier, RANGER. Threats to peace until this time had been concentrated in Europe and the Middle East.

As world tensions increased the Soviet and Communist Chinese submarine forces were becoming an increasing threat. But at this time the Navy was reducing to ten its Anti-Submarine Warfare (ASW) carriers with the mothballing of most straight deck ESSEX carriers. The last Escort Carrier (CVE) was mothballed by 1957 with the exception of four which were reclassified as Helicopter Escort Carriers (CVHEs) or Utility Carriers (CVUs) used to transport aircraft.

By July of 1958 there were seven super carriers authorized. These carriers with their fifty plus attack bombers were a component of the US nuclear strike force. But with the advent of the ICBM the opponents of the aircraft carrier were again becoming vocal with cries of *high cost* and *obsolescence*. These attacks were a repeat of the post war rhetoric; ... *why carriers when we have other means, and besides they are vulnerable to aircraft with missiles.* An especially scathing attack was expressed by the head of the Appropriations Committee of The House of Representatives who pointed out that '... Russia has been too wise to build a single carrier'. He concluded from this that the reason for the US deficiency in submarines, missiles and overall military power was the fault of building carriers. Representative Cannon mustered enough votes to have the House drop a new carrier but the Senate forced a compromise only to have President Eisenhower refuse to let the Navy spend the funds! Finally in July of 1960 both Congress and the President agreed to a new carrier with conventional power.

As FORRESTAL carriers entered service ESSEX carriers, less suited for jet operations, were reclassified as ASW carriers (CVS). The ASW carriers

(Above) F4D-1 Skyray of VF-13 Aggressors approaching ESSEX (CVA-9) while deployed to the Med in January of 1960. The new angled deck adopted by the Navy for its attack carriers permitted jet aircraft to maintain full power during landing approaches permitting a go around if they had a bolter. (USN)

were maintained at ten, nine for ASW work, and the tenth to serve as a training carrier. At the end of 1963 the fifteen CVAs in service included seven of the new FORRESTAL class, three MIDWAY class , and five ESSEX class.

(Below) S2F-3 Trackers of VS-36 and VS-26 taxiing to launch from RANDOLPH (CVS-15) during 1962. Originally an Essex class CVA, RANDOLPH was redesignated a CVS in March of 1959. (Grumman)

(Below) F11F-1 (141811) Tiger of VF-33 Astronauts tied down aboard INTREPID (CVA-11) in June of 1960, during VF-33's second deployment with F11Fs. The A4D-2 Skyhawks are from VA-66 (AF-302) and VA-76 (AF-503/504). (USN)

CARRIER AIR GROUPS

ATTACK CARRIER AIR GROUPS (CVG/ATG) - The number of CVGs remained nearly constant during the 1957 to 1963 period. Air Task Groups had received their squadrons by transferring in one squadron from the Fleet CVGs which now were reduced from six fighter and attack squadrons to five. With the arrival of the super carriers, and reduced squadron size Air Task Groups (ATG) were phased out by 1960.

(Above) AD-6 (137495) Skyraider of VA-196 Flying Devils as part of ATG-1 just prior to deployment aboard TICONDEROGA (CVA-14) in October of 1958. ATG-1 was disestablished at the conclusion of the cruise in February of 1959. (Bill Larkins)

REPLACEMENT CARRIER AIR GROUPS (RCVG) - Post War carrier replacement training was scheduled to that of carrier deployments which resulted in air groups deploying with replacement pilots often having to get their readiness training after the beginning of a deployment. This self training often took eighteen to twenty-four months and coupled with the introduction of the new jets resulted in soaring accident rates. Effective 10 April 1958, the Chief of Naval Operations (CNO) adopted a reorganization plan that contained the following:

1. Create two Replacement Carrier Air Groups (RCVG), one for each coast that consolidated all attack carrier training within these groups. They would be similar in mission to the WWII Advance Carrier Training Groups. They were normally referred to as Replacement Air Groups (RAGs).
2. Reduce Fleet squadron's responsibility in the indoctrination of replacement pilots.
3. Standardize tactics and maintenance procedures.
4. Fleet squadrons converting to new aircraft will come under the supervision of RCVGs until the Fleet Introduction Program (FIP) transition syllabus is completed.
5. Dissolve the present Heavy Attack Wing structure by assigning a VAH squadron or detachment (DET) to each CVG.

Those commands evolved in various phases of advanced indoctrination were absorbed by those Fleet squadrons assigned to the new RCVGs. Assigned squadrons used the tail codes of their respective RCVG. RCVG-4 (AD) was designated for the Atlantic Fleet and RCVG-12 (NJ) for the Pacific Fleet.

(Above) A4D-2N (148455) CAG Skyhawk of VA-66 Waldomen in May of 1961. They had returned in February from a Med cruise aboard INTREPID (CVA-11). Squadron numbers were 3OO series with Blue trim. (Larry Smalley)

ASW CARRIER AIR GROUPS (CVSG) - The first two CVSGs were commissioned in April of 1960 and were followed by eight additional groups over the next nine months. This resulted in new squadrons being commissioned to permit one CVSG for each ASW carrier. With this reorganization individual VS and HS squadron tail codes became obsolete. With the introduction of the new CVSGs, effective 11 May 1960, a set of two digit squadron nose numbers were issued along with trim colors.

(Above) S-2D (S2F-3) (148718) of VS-37 Patient Professionals deploying with sister squadrons VS-35, HS-2, and a DET of VAW-11 aboard HORNET (CVS-14) in October of 1963. (USN)

REPLACEMENT ASW CARRIER AIR GROUPS (RCVSG) - The success of the new RCVG training scheme was paying such handsome dividends for the attack carrier operations that it was expanded to the field of ASW training. This was initially achieved on 30 June 1960 when two replacement ASW air groups (CVSGs) were established. These RCVSGs were referred to as ASW RAGs.

(Below) A4D-1 Skyhawks of VA-44 Blackbirds adopted a Blue fuselage arrow design scattered with White stars in 1958. (MDAC via Harry Gann)

CARRIER AIR GROUP LINEAGE

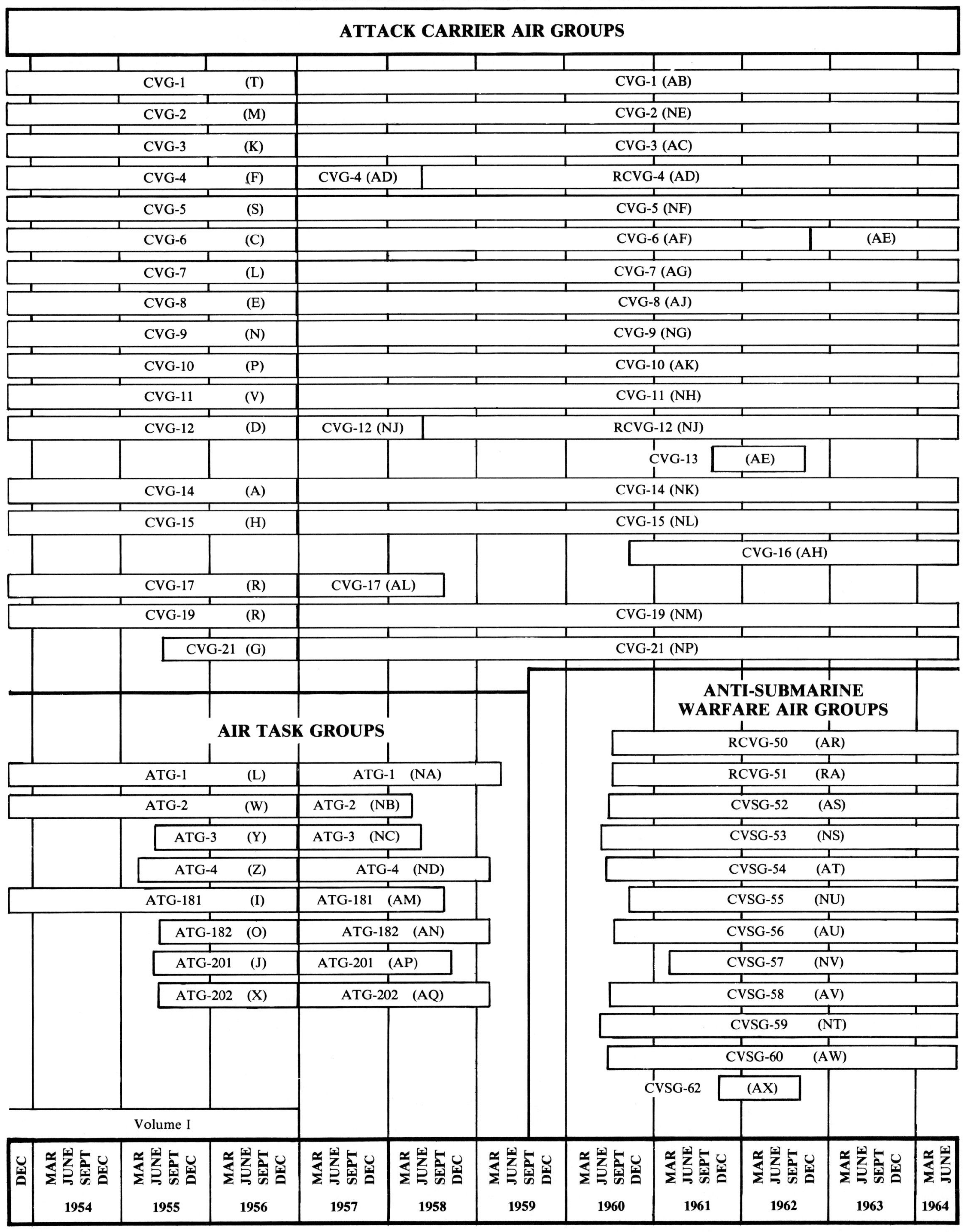

AIRCRAFT COLORS

The Glossy Sea Blue, often referred to as Dark Blue, introduced during WWII had proven too conspicuous and alternate color schemes had been under evaluation from 1953 to 1955. One of the earliest experiments was with a bare metal finish, but it was not acceptable. The scheme finally selected in February of 1955 was Light Gull Gray (sometimes referred to as a Matt Sea Gull Gray) applied to the top and sides of aircraft over Glossy White (officially called Insignia White) on the under surfaces. Insignia White was also applied to the upper sides of the control surfaces. Light Gull Gray had been selected for the upper surfaces as the least conspicuous at altitude and Insignia White was selected for the under surfaces to provide a reflective finish from the heat and flash of a nuclear device. Those aircraft still painted in Sea Blue were to conform to the new scheme by 1 July 1957. Many carrier squadrons operated aircraft in both color schemes through this transition period. Glossy Sea Blue was retained on shore based command aircraft. Engine Gray was selected for helicopters in the utility role. Those helicopters deployed aboard carriers were normally painted in overall Gull Gray, but on 27 December 1961 Engine Gray was ordered for both ASW and Utility helicopter squadrons.

(Above) F9F-8B (138830) Cougar of VA-126 Trailblazers in Glossy Sea Blue carrying a two digit nose number at Miramar in August of 1957. VA-126 was transitioning to the FJ-4 Fury at this time and the Cougar was apparently used as a training aircraft. The rest of CVG-12 was deployed aboard LEXINGTON (CVA-16). (Bill Larkins)

(Above) A-3B (A3D-2) of VAH-11 Checkertails refueling a F-3B (F3H-2) Demon of VF-14 Tophatters while an RF-8A (F8U-1P) Crusader of VFP-62 awaits its turn during a flight from ROOSEVELT (CVA-42) in March of 1963. The Gull Gray over Insignia White scheme allowed squadrons to adopt colorful trim color designs. (USN)

(Below) SH-34Gs (HSS-1) of HS-6 parked at Barbers Point during October of 1962. They deployed with KEARSARGE (CVS-33). The colors are Engine Gray with Orange nose trim and a Yellow band on the tail rotor section. (USN)

(Below) FJ-3Ds from GMGRU-1 during the change over from Glossy Sea Blue to Light Gull Gray over Insignia White. GMGRU-1 supplied drone/missile controllers in support of the Fleet, supplying DETs to CVAs to serve as missile controllers for the Regulas missile. Near Barbers Point in 1960. (USN via Fred Roos)

HIGH VISIBILITY - With the establishment of the Light Gull Gray over Insignia White aircraft color scheme during 1956 mid-air safety became a concern. In July of 1956 aircraft used by training units were directed to use Insignia White overall with an International Orange 'split' paint scheme to increase mid-air visibility. International Orange was often referred to as Day-Glo Orange, and was also developed in a solvent removable type of paint which could be removed without affecting the tactical finish underneath. The International Orange, used for carrier training, was more lasting and not used by tactical units. International Orange trim was applied along the wings, nose, tail and fuselage on fixed wing aircraft. On helicopters it was applied to the nose, tail section and pylons. For carrier based tactical aircraft, only those aircraft within the various RAGs were painted in International Orange. In a directive issued on 30 April 1959 International Orange was replaced by Florescent Red Orange. The tactical CVG/ATG commanders had the option of applying it when operating in the CONUS. Actual application varied considerably for training aircraft and few tactical commanders used the highly visible International Orange or Red Orange paint.

A second high visibility scheme that was only rarely seen in tactical squadrons occurred when utility squadrons (VU) loaned an aircraft to a tactical squadron for special duties. Examples are aircraft employed as tugs for towing target sleeves and aerial target control aircraft. These aircraft were painted with Orange Yellow wings, vertical elevator, and horizontal stabilizers; the rudder was painted Insignia Red; the fuselage in Engine Gray. A 36 inch wide Insignia Red band was painted chordwise on both surfaces of the wings. In December of 1959 Insignia Red was changed to Florescent Red Orange with the vertical fin painted in the same color.

(Above) F9F-8T (142471) Cougar trainer of VF-111 Sundowners in the overall Glossy White aircraft with International Orange trim used for high visibility by training squadrons. This Cougar was an interim utility aircraft used by the Sundowners while shore based at Miramar during 1957. (Jim Sullivan Collection)

(Above Right) A-1E (AD-5) (133907) Skyraider of VAW-33 Night Hawkers aboard ESSEX (CVS-9) during 1963 in the utility aircraft scheme of Orange Yellow wings and fixed surfaces. The cowl is also trimmed in Yellow. The fuel tanks are White with Red circles, while the rest of the aircraft is Engine Gray. (Duane Kasulka Collection)

(Right) A3D-2 (135432) of VAH-3 Sea Dragons at George AFB in May of 1960. This A3D is in the tactical Gull Gray and Insignia White scheme, but has added International Orange trim authorized for tactical aircraft when in CONUS. (Larry Kasulka)

(Below) AD-6 (142075) Skyraider of VA-96 as part of ATG-3 which was deployed aboard KEARSARGE (CVA-31) from August of 1957 through April of 1958. This unlucky pilot landed aboard SHANGRI LA (CVA-38) and CVG-11 crew members did the honor of letting him show off their handy work. The wing tips and fuselage band of International Orange are the high visibility markings employed by tactical squadrons during training or 'qual' cruises. (Tailhook)

CVG/ATG TRIM COLORS AND AIRCRAFT NUMBERS - With the introduction of the new Gray over White color scheme squadron trim colors for CVA Air Groups were revised on 9 March 1955. The trend towards colorfully marked aircraft reached its height. Large fuselage bands and chevrons were added, tail surfaces, nose sections, wing tips, etc all received splashes of the squadron's trim color. This often led to squadrons adopting their trim colors into the squadron insignia in bold sizes. Squadron insignias had been used before, but had usually been rather inconspicuous due to their size and the Sea Blue aircraft color. Squadron insignias grew in size and many WWII insignias were resurected and used since the original squadron had been disestablished leaving the insignia up for grabs. Air group trim colors had shade variations and the Orange Yellow (2xx) often looked like an Orange, while the Orange (4xx) often looked like a Red (1xx). Provisions for a special block of numbers being reserved for the CVG Commander was discontinued and the use of even hundred numbers (100, 200, 300, etc) became official. This was actually more of a paper change since the system had been in use since the early 1950s. In recognition of the growing importance of support squadrons to the CVG/ATG on 23 December 1958 a directive was released that assigned six, seven, eight, and nine hundred block numbers to VAH,

VAW, VA(AW) and VFP squadrons respectively. DETS retained the 1 to 99 series. Atlantic Fleet (LANT) squadrons followed the hundred series for both squadrons and DETs. The Pacific Fleet (PAC) followed the directive more closely, using the 1 through 99 normally for DETs and only the hundred series for full squadrons of VA and VF.

The application of these aircraft numbers and trim colors were followed as a general rule, but within an Air Group they varied; often a DET would apply its own choice of colors with the CAG Commanding Officer usually permitting variations in the assignment of nose numbers. Prior squadron designation and the corresponding aircraft nose number scheme had already began to breakdown. Often in an effort to follow the 1948 directive (see Volume I) squadrons were redesignated when they moved to a new Air Group which required a new set of aircraft nose numbers with corresponding trim color changes. When there was a change in CVG squadrons, each squadron was renumbered with the senior squadron becoming the first squadron carrying the 100 series nose numbers and the others aligning themselves on the basis of seniority within the CVG regardless of the squadron type. ATGs followed a similar method. Other squadrons simply accepted vacated nose number series.

(Above) F8U-1 (143714) Crusader of VF-211 Red Checkertails in their colorful Red and White checkered tail and a Red arrow along the fuselage. Miramar during August of 1960. (Warren Bodie)

(Below) A4D-2 (142685) of VA-12 Flying Ubangis at Miami in January of 1958 after converting from the F7U Cutlass. They were reassigned to CVG-10 shortly after this but did not deploy until 1960. (Bill Swisher)

(Above) F4D-1 (134876) of VF-141 carrying a Yellow banner on the tail about to be catapulted from BON HOMME RICHARD (CVA-31) during a WestPac cruise in late 1957. (MDAC)

(Below) A-5A (148925) Vigilante of VAH-7 Peacemakers during carrier 'quals' with CVG-6 aboard ENTERPRISE (CVAN-65) in 1962. They would later adopt a 700 nose number series and the 'AF' tail code of CVG-6. (USN)

(Above) AD-6 (139701) of VA-145 Swordsmen at Miramar back from a cruise aboard HORNET (CVA-12) in July of 1958. At this time the squadrons of CVG-14 all had similar tail designs. (Doug Olson via Bill Swisher)

CVG/ATG SQUADRON TRIM COLORS AND AIRCRAFT NUMBERS

	March 1955		Dec 1958	
X00's	Multi-Colors		CAG	No change
101 & Up	Insignia Red		VF	No change
201 & Up	Orange Yellow		VF	No change
301 & Up	Light Blue		VF*	No change
401 & Up	International Orange		VA	No change
501 & Up	Light Green		VA	No change
601 & Up	Black		VAH	601 & Up
			VAW	701 & Up
			VA(AW)	801 & Up
			VFP	901 & Up
1 to 99	Maroon		DETs	No change

*Evolved with improved jets to an attack squadron.

(Below) EA-1F (AD-5Q) (132618) Skyraider of VAW-33 Night Hawkers aboard ENTERPRISE (CVAN-65) during 1963. East Coast DETs used 100 series nose numbers which was formally established in December of 1958. (USN)

(Below) UH-2A (HU2K-1) (149739) of HU-1 Fleet Angels aboard TICONDEROGA (CVA-14) in Engine Gray. DETs used a 1 through 99 series of aircraft nose numbers. (Harry Gann)

(Below) A-3B (A3D-2) (142403) Skywarrior of VAH-8 Fireballers at North Island in April of 1963. VAH-8 deployed aboard MIDWAY (CVA-41) in November for a WestPac cruise, their fifth aboard the MIDWAY. (Clay Jansson)

(Above) E-1B (148143) of VAW-11, DET-F of CVG-14 deployed aboard CONSTELLATION (CVA-64) during 1963. VAW squadrons, especially those on the West Coast rarely applied trim colors or CVG tail codes. (Toda Koda)

(Below) F9F-8P (144421) Cougar of VFP-62 engaged the crash barrier aboard ESSEX (CVA-9) in July of 1959. Photo squadrons used 900 series numbers which was officially set down by the 1958 directive, however the 900 series numbers had been in limited usage since the mid 1950s. (USN)

11

CVSG/RCVSG TRIM COLORS AND AIRCRAFT NUMBERS -Carrier based anti-submarine warfare air groups (CVSG) were established in April of 1960 with trim colors being assigned the following month. Prior to this ASW squadrons had used what ever colors suited them. Aircraft nose numbers were also assigned to the squadrons that now made up these new CVSGs.

(Below) S-2F (S2F-1S1) (136506) of VS-24 Duty Cats with magnetic airborne detector (MAD) gear extended from the tail during an ASW exercise off the coast of Virginia in 1963. Trim colors are Red and White. (USN)

CVSG SQUADRON TRIM COLORS AND AIRCRAFT NUMBERS

MAY 1960			
1st Sqd	10 to 29	VS	Insignia Red
2nd Sqd	30 to 59	VS	Orange Yellow
3rd Sqd	60 to 79	HS	Light Blue
DET*	80 to 99		Maroon

*Beginning in 1963 VA DETs were added for Combat Air Protection using a 1 through 9 number series with Red trim colors.

(Above) S-2B (S2F-1S) (136658) of VS-29, the second squadron within CVSG-53, in December of 1962. Trim colors are Yellow with Black stripes. (USN)

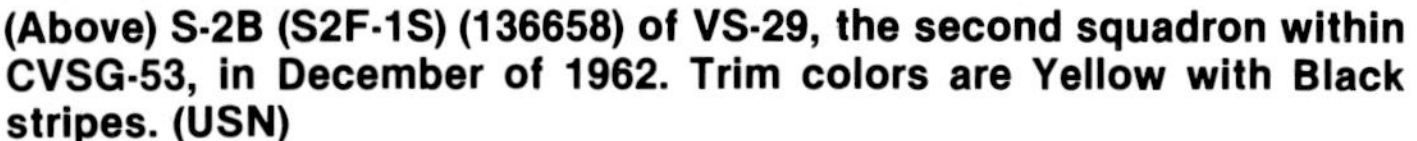

(Below) A-4B (A4D-2) (132676) Skyraider of VMA-214, DET-N attached to CVSG-57 for HORNET's (CVS-12) cruise in late 1963. Skyhawk DETs were added to CVSGs to provide limited air protection for the carrier and its air group. (Clay Jansson)

(Above) HSS-1N (148957) of HS-8 at Ream Field in August of 1962. The Engine Gray with International Orange trim was adopted for carrier ASW helicopter squadrons in 1961. (Bill Swisher)

(Below) AD-5W (132743) Skyraider of VAW-12 DET about to deploy aboard ESSEX (CVS-9) during 1960. The Maroon trim color is carried in a Bat design behind the codes on the tail, the 700 series nose numbers are a carry over from those used by DETs aboard CVAs. (Roger Besecker)

BERLIN CRISIS

Soviet pressure on the city of Berlin climaxed in mid-August of 1961 when the communists began erecting what would become known as "The Berlin Wall". President Kennedy reacted by increasing the readiness of US armed forces.

FLEET COMMISSIONINGS - For the Fleet this included increasing the carrier force from fourteen to fifteen CVAs, adding an attack carrier air group (CVG-13) and an ASW air group (CVSG-62) with their new squadrons. CVG-13 was added to the Atlantic Fleet and assigned to the new super carrier CONSTELLATION. The following year when the CONSTELLATION was transferred to the Pacific Fleet after stabilization of the Berlin Crisis, the need for a sixteenth Carrier Air Group was not justified, and CVG-13 and its squadrons was disestablished on 1 October 1962; the same logic preceded the disestablishment of CVSG-62.

An interesting story on how CVG-6 got its tail codes has been related. While several US Senators were observing carrier operations of CVG-6 squadrons (then carrying tail codes of 'AF'). Indicating the 'AF' tail codes,

(Above) AD-6 (137497) Skyraider of VA-135 Thunderbirds catching an arresting cable on the newly commissioned CONSTELLATION (CVA-64) in December of 1962. Before VA-135 was disestablished they had 1500 safe traps on four CVAs. (USN via Pete Bowers)

one of the Senators wondered what all the Air Force aircraft were doing aboard a Navy carrier? Orders to change CVG-6's tail codes were swift in coming, and was made easier with the disestablishment of CVG-13. CVG-13's tail code 'AE' was reassigned to CVG-6.

FLEET COMMISSIONINGS

Air Station	CVG-13	AE		Air Station	CVSG-62	AX	
Cecil Field	VF-131	F-3B	100	Quonset Point	VS-20	S-2F	10
Cecil Field	VF-132	F-8D	200	Quonset Point	VS-42	S-2B	30
Cecil Field	VA-133	A-4B	300	Quonset Point	HS-13	SH-34J	60
Cecil Field	VA-134	A-4B	400	—	—	—	—
Jacksonville	VA-135	A-1H	500	—	—	—	—
Whidbey Island	VAH-10	A-3B	600	—	—	—	—

VAW-12 and VFP-63 supplied DETs for CONSTELLATION during its shake down cruise in early 1961 as part of CVG-13.

RESERVE CALLUPS - On 1 October 1961 the President of the United States called up eighteen Naval Reserve squadrons, five patrol squadrons (VPs) and thirteen carrier ASW squadrons (VSs) equipped with S2F-1s (S-2As) to supplement the Fleets ASW capability. These reserves were released the following summer on 1 August.

RESERVE CALLUP

Reserve Station		
Glenview	VS-721	SY
Grosse Ile	VS-733	CT
Lakehurst	VS-751	CQ
Los Alamitos	VS-771	ST
Los Alamitos	VS-772	SU
New Orleans	VS-821	CU
New York	VS-837	CR
Norfolk	VS-861	CV
Alameda	VS-872	SW
Alameda	VS-873	SV
Washington	VS-891	SX
Willow Grove	VS-935	CP
South Weymouth	VS-915	CS

(Above) F3H-2 (136996) Demon of VF-131 at Oceana during 1962. VF-131 was assigned to CONSTELLATION (CVA-64) as part of the added force level activated during the Berlin Wall crisis. (MDAC via Fred Harl)

(Below) S2F-1 (133241) of VS-935 was activated from Willow Grove during 1962. The Liberty Bells carried on the rudder are Yellow on a Black field. (Fred Roos Collection)

(Above) F3H-2 (143079) Demon of VF-41 Black Aces at Yuma in December of 1959 carrying CAG colors and squadron trim colors of Red which includes the carrier name. INDEPENDENCE (CVA-62) at this time was the Navy's newest carrier and had just completed its shakedown cruise in September. (Bill Swisher)

(Left) A4D-2N (147771) of VA-192 Golden Dragons with the squadron trim color of Yellow at Norton AFB in May of 1962. VA-192 deployed aboard BON HOMME RICHARD (CVA-31) in July of 1962. (Bill Swisher)

(Below) AD-5 (133858) Skyraider of VA-52 at Miramar in 1959. The use of a utility aircraft such as the AD-5 was common for tactical squadrons when shore based. (Dusty Carter via Bill Larkins)

(Left) F8U-2 (146931) Crusader of VF-124 Moonshiners at Yuma in March of 1960. Trim is Orange in keeping with the fourth squadron within a CVG. The squadron was based at Miramar for F8U Fleet crew training. (Bill Swisher via Clay Jansson)

(Below) AD-6 (139701) Skyraider of VA-165 Boomers carrying the colorful CAG chevrons at Moffett Field in May of 1962 just a month before they deployed aboard ORISKANY (CVA-34) to the Pacific. (Bill Larkins)

COMMANDER (CAG)

(Above) A3D-2s (138906/CAG) of VAH-13 jettisoning fuel near San Diego in December of 1961. They are part of CVG-11 working on KITTYHAWK's (CVA-63) shakedown. (USN)

(Right) A4D-2 (142420) Skyhawk of VA-12 Flown by Cdr Bill Barrow at Yuma in 1958. Carrier name is in Red with Blue and Yellow trim colors outlined in Black. The Blue is a result of VA-12 being the third squadron in CVG-10, and the Yellow stems from their original colors when they were the second squadron as denoted by the 2 in the designator. (MDAC)

(Below) S2F-1 (136483) of CVSVG-60 taxiing forward for launch from ESSEX (CVS-9) in 1960. The use of "double nuts" for ASW aircraft was rare at this time. (USN)

(Right) TF-9J (147312) Cougar from CAG-12 in the Gloss White with the International Orange trim that was used on aircraft assigned to RAG training squadrons. The aircraft belongs to VA-126 which provided instrument training. Miramar January of 1963. (Clay Jansson)

(Below) F4D-1 (134870) Skyray of VF-101 after landing aboard FOR-RESTAL (CVA-59) in May of 1960. Trim colors are Red with White diamonds. (USN via Nick Williams)

MARINE CORPS SQUADRONS

Marine fighter and attack squadrons are periodically carrier qualified and often operate aboard carriers inplace of Navy squadrons. This normally took place when a Navy squadron was in transition to a new aircraft type or when there was a need to temporarily expand carrier tactical air power. Marine carrier assignments reached a high of five squadrons during the Berlin Wall crisis of 1961/62. By the early 1960s the method of squadron identification was well established with the Marine Corps squadrons adopting the Navy CVG tail code and numbering system. Beginning in 1963 the first Marine DET was attached to a CVSG to provide a limited Combat Air Patrol (CAP) fighter protection for the defenseless CVS and her aircraft. Those Marine squadrons known to have deployed as part of a carrier air group in this time period are listed below.

(Above) F4D-1 (139035) Skyray of VMFAW-115 attached to CVG-1 awaiting launch on the deck of ROOSEVELT (CVA-42) in April of 1959. Marine Corps squadrons attached were now adopting the CVG's tail code and trim color scheme. (USN)

(Above) F8U-1E (145460) of VMF-251 at South Weymouth in September of 1962. The squadron was attached to CVG-10 aboard the SHANGRI-LA (CVA-38). (Roger Besecker Collection)

(Left) F8U-2 (145595) Crusader of VMF-323 Death Rattlers at Ontario, CA in May of 1962. They had just returned from a cruise aboard LEXINGTON (CVA-16) as part of CVG-14. They retained their own squadron tail code during this cruise, but trim color was Yellow in keeping with the second squadron within a CVG. (Duane Kasulka)

(Below) A4D-2 (142731) of VMA-225 refueling a CAG-10 FJ-3M from VF-62. The Fury is carrying the CVW-10 insignia on the vertical fin, and the VF-62 insignia below the canopy. (USN)

(Below) F4D-1 Skyrays of VMFAW-115 off INDEPENDENCE (CVA-62) during 1962. This was the third cruise of INDEPENDENCE, all to the Med. (USN via Nick Williams)

MARINE CORPS DEPLOYMENTS with CARRIER AIR GROUPS (1957-1963)						
Sqdn	**Aircraft**		**ID**	**Air Groups**	**Carrier**	**Deploy Date**
VMFAW-114	F4D-1	Skyray	AB-200	CVG-1	ROOSEVELT	2/59-9/59
VMFAW-115	F4D-1	Skyray	AG-100	CVG-7	INDEPENDENCE	4/62-8/62
VMA-121	A4D-2	Skyhawk	NL-400	CVG-15	CORAL SEA	9/60-5/61
VMFAW-214	F2H-4	Banshee	WE-300	ATG-2	HANCOCK	4/57-9/57
VMA-214	A-4B	Skyhawk	WK-80	CVSG-57	HORNET	10/63-4/64
VMA-224	A4D-2	Skyhawk	AG-500	CVG-7	INDEPENDENCE	8/60-3/61
VMA-225	A4D-2	Skyhawk	AK-500	CVG-10	ESSEX	7/59-2/60
VMA-225	A4D-2N	Skyhawk	AK-600	CVG-10	SHANGRI LA	2/61-5/61
VMA-225	A-4C	Skyhawk	AE-600	CVG-6	ENTERPRISE	10/62-11/62
VMA-225	A-4C	Skyhawk	AK-600	CVG-10	SHANGRI LA	10/63-4/64
VMF-232	F8U-1NE	Crusader	WT-200	CVG-16	ORISKANY	6/62-12/62
VMF-251	F8U-1NE	Crusader	AK-200	CVG-10	SHANGRI LA	2/62-8/62
VMF-323	F8U-2	Crusader	WS-200	CVG-14	LEXINGTON	11/61-5/62
VMA-324	A4D-2	Skyhawk	NL-100	CVG-15	CORAL SEA	2/61-5/61
VMA-324	A-4B	Skyhawk	AG-500	CVG-7	INDEPENDENCE	8/63-3/64
VMFAW-533	F2H-4	Banshee	ED-00	ATG-182	LAKE CHAMPLAIN	1/57-7/57

VMA-121 and VMA-324 based at Atsugi, Japan replaced CVG-15's fighter squadrons from February through May 1961.

ATTACK CARRIER SQUADRONS

In the mid-1950s the Navy began to revise the composition of its attack carrier air groups (CVG/ATG). Early in WWII the Navy had replaced bombers with fighters and by the time of the Korean War there were three or four fighter squadrons to each attack squadron in the CVGs and ATGs. This was possible because the Hellcat, Corsair, and Bearcat possessed ground attack capability. While US policy, even after the Korean War, centered on the thesis that there would be no major conflict without the use of nuclear weapons, it was only with the arrival of the super carriers and high performance jets in the late 1950s that the CVG's composition was restructured to increase attack aircraft squadrons. This evolved into two fighter squadrons, one all-weather intercepter squadron (F4D Skyrays, F3H Demons or F4H Phantom IIs), and one day fighter squadron (F9F-8 Cougars, FJ-4 Furys, or F8U Crusaders). Next each CVG/ATG was assigned either one or two light attack jet squadrons (FJ-4B Furys, F9F-8B Cougars, or A4D Skyhawks). In addition each CVG/ATG had a medium attack squadron equipped with the AD Skyraider and some air groups aboard the super carriers carried a second AD squadron. The CVG/ATG aboard MIDWAY and FORRESTAL class carriers had yet an additional squadron of heavy attack aircraft (AJ Savages or A3D Skywarriors).

FIGHTER AND ATTACK AIRCRAFT

The beginning of 1957 saw Fleet fighter and attack squadrons flying nine major aircraft types in eighty-five squadrons. By the end of 1964 only three types remained that had been in service seven years earlier.

F7U CUTLASS - The Chance Vought F7U-3 Cutlass, first introduced in 1954, equipped seven squadrons at the beginning of 1957. With its planned replacement available only one squadron operated the Cutlass beyond July of 1957 and adopted the newly assigned double tail letters that were mandatory after this date. The Cutlass had been operated in both the attack and fighter role as the F7U-3, and the missile equipped F7U-3M, before being phased out by VA-116 in late 1957.

(Below) F7U-3M (139917) Cutlass of VA-116 being launched from HANCOCK (CVA-19) in 1957. VA-116 was the last operational Fleet Cutlass squadron, this was the last Cutlass built. (USN)

F2H (F-2) BANSHEE - The last of the straight wing jets, the McDonnell F2H Banshee was introduced in 1949, and remained as the F2H-3 and F2H-4 (F-2C and F-2D) all-weather interceptor. The Banshee was replaced by the all-weather McDonnell F3H Demon and other newer jets until only VF-92 was left with the all-weather F2H-3. VF-92 began converting to the F3H Demon in September of 1958.

(Right) F2H-3 (127533) Banshee of VF-154 at Moffett Field in May of 1957. VF-154 had operated the Banshee since 1954 and after their 1958 cruise transitioned to the Skyraider. (Bill Larkins via Pete Bowers)

(Above) F2H-3 (126419) Banshee of VF-92 aboard YORKTOWN (CVA-10) in July of 1958. In September VF-92 deployed aboard TICONDEROGA (CVA-14) to WestPac. (Doug Olson via Bill Larkins)

(Below) F2H-4 (126417) of VA-152 Aces, newly designated as an attack squadron for this cruise aboard BENNINGTON (CVA-10). This was their sixth Banshee cruise and upon completing it in January of 1959 they converted to the AD Skyraider. (USN via Fred Roos)

(Above) F2H-3 (126474) of VF-52 at Moffett Field in May of 1958. In October VF-52 deployed to the Western Pacific aboard TICONDEROGA (CVA-14) as part of ATG-4 which was disestablished in February of 1959 upon their return. (Bill Larkins)

(Below) F2H-3 (127578/98) of VF-11 Red Rippers somewhere in the Mediterranean during a 1958 cruise aboard ESSEX (CVA-9). They would return in November of 1958 at which time ATG-201 was disestablished. (USN)

F9F (F-9) COUGAR - The swept-wing Grumman F9F-6 (F-9F) Cougar was phased out of the Fleet in early 1957 by VA-156. The improved F9F-8 (F-9J) Cougar interceptor carried four Sidewinder missiles to supplement its four 20ᴍᴍ cannons, and the attack version of the Cougar the F9F-8B (AF-9J) was equipped with a low altitude bombing system for carrying nuclear bombs. Those squadrons equipped with the F9F-8B were normally designated attack squadrons. At the beginning of 1957 there were twenty-seven Cougar squadrons, and by 1958 the Cougar was phased out of the Pacific Fleet, and by mid 1959 VA-76 of the Atlantic Fleet had phased out the last Cougar.

(Right) F9F-8 (141177) Cougar of VA-36 Road Runners during September of 1958. VA-36 did not deploy with ATG-201 in February but remained in CONUS. (Roger Besecker Collection)

(Above) F9F-8B (141118) Cougar of VF-94 in ATG-4 markings at Moffett Field in June of 1957. The Cougar was being rapidly phased out, as were the ATGs they were assigned to. (Bill Larkins via Clay Jansson)

(Below) F9F-8 (144301) of VF-144 Knight Riders at Miramar in August of 1957 just back from a cruise aboard HORNET (CVA-12) in July. Trim color is Orange with White 'NK' CVG-14 tail code. The squadron was later redesignated VA-52 in February of 1959. (Larry Smally)

(Above) F9F-8B Cougars of VA-56 over California in June of 1957. VA-56 did not deploy on BON HOMME RICHARD (CVA-31) when CVG-5 deployed in July since they were to begin transitioning to the FJ-4 Fury. (USN)

(Below) F9F-8 (131081) of VF-13 Aggressors at Cecil Field in November of 1958 carrying CVG-17 tail codes. CVG-17 had been disestablished in September and VF-13 is awaiting new aircraft and assignment to an existing CVG. (Via Jim Sullivan)

AD (A-1) SKYRAIDER - The Douglas AD Skyraider, introduced in 1949, had evolved into the -6 (A-1H), and the -7 (A-1J). The AD-6 featured improved low level bombing capability, and the AD-7 had strengthened wings and landing gear. The number of carrier squadrons operating the Skyraider reached a high of twenty squadrons in 1958 when the FJ-4B and F9F-8B began limited replacement of the Skyraider until there was only one AD squadron per CVG/CVW in the early 1960s. When shored based AD squadrons normally operated the AD-5 (A-1E) for utility duties.

(Below) AD-6 (139817) Skyraider of VA-176 Thunderbolts at Yuma in 1958 as part of CVG-17. CVG-17 was disestablished in September, with VA-176 being re-assigned to CVG-10. (MDAC)

(Above) AD-6 (137549) Skyraider of VA-66 Waldomen taking off from INTREPID (CVA-11) during a 1960 Med cruise. CVG-6 markings included the familiar six stars on the rudder and a thunderbolt on the fuselage. (Pete Bowers)

(Above) AD-6 (135370) of VA-115 Chargers at Moffett Field after having just completed a cruise aboard ESSEX (CVA-9) in May of 1957. (Clay Jansson)

(Left) AD-6 (137551) Skyraider of VA-42 Green Pawns in ATG-181 markings with Orange and Black trim colors. The squadron insignia, a Green Pawn, is painted on the engine cowl both above and below the aircraft nose number. VA-42 was assigned to ATG-181 just prior to its disestablishment in August of 1958. (Roger Besecker)

(Below) A1-H (137537) Skyraider of VA-196 at Lemoore, in July of 1963. (Clay Jansson)

(Above) AD-6 (137585) of VA-105 refueling an A4D-2 (142133) of VA-83 during cruise to the Med aboard ESSEX (CVA-9) in April of 1958 as part of ATG-201. Deployed from the US in February of 1958, upon their return in November ATG-201 was disestablished. (USN)

(Below) AD-6 Skyraiders of VA-145 Swordsmen in a new marking scheme at the Fleet Air Weapons Meet at El Centro in April of 1958. The Swordsmen flew cross country to Norfolk the following month to board RANGER (CVA-61) for a cruise around Cape Horn to San Diego. (USN)

(Above) AD-6 (137534) of VA-215 at Alameda in May of 1958 carrying the checkerboard tail design used by the squadrons of CVG-21. (Larry Smalley)

(Below) AD-6 (139750) of VA-96 at Alameda in May of 1958 awaiting O&R. VA-96 had just returned from a cruise aboard TICONDEROGA (CVA-14) at which time ATG-3 and VA-96 were both disestablished. (Larry Smalley)

(Above) AD-7 (142029) Skyraider of VA-216 carrying ATG-4 markings at Moffett Field in June of 1957. They deployed in January of 1958 aboard HORNET (CVA-12) to the Pacific. (Larry Smalley)

FJ (F-1) FURY - The North American Fury initially reached the Fleet in early 1954 as the FJ-2 variant but was unacceptable to the Navy and resulted in a new design under the designation FJ-3 (F-1C) with increased underwing pylons making it an excellent ground attack aircraft. Another version was the FJ-3M (MF-1C) which was equipped with the Sidewinder missile. The FJ-3 and FJ-3M were so successful that 1957 saw 23 Navy and Marine squadrons flying them. The next version was the FJ-4 (F-1E) designed as a day fighter interceptor while the FJ-4B (AF-1E) was an attack version with nuclear capability and provisions for four air-to-ground Bullpup missiles. The first deployment of the nuclear Bullpup was with VA-212 in 1959 to WestPac. A total of ten attack squadrons received the FJ-4B. The last Fury was phased out by the Black Diamonds of VA-216 in late 1962.

(Right) FJ-3 (135928) Fury of VF-154 at Moffett Field in mid 1957 with Orange trim. They began conversion to the F8U Crusader the following year. (Bill Larkins)

(Above) FJ-3 (135943) of VF-91 Red Lightings in the markings used by the squadrons of CVG-9. VF-91 had just completed a cruise aboard TICONDEROGA (CVA-14) in April of 1958. (Bill Larkins)

(Below) FJ-3M (141395) of VF-142 with Blue and White trim at Miramar in August of 1957. They continued to use Blue rather than the prescribed Yellow. (Larry Smalley)

(Above) FJ-4 (136072) of VF-62 in storage at Litchfield in March of 1960. Their last cruise with the Fury was completed aboard ESSEX (CVA-9) in early 1960. (Bill Swisher)

(Below) FJ-4B (143571) of VA-63 being launched from MIDWAY (CVA-41) in January of 1959. VA-63 had converted from the F9F-8 Cougar to the Fury the year before. After this cruise they were redesignated to VA-22 in July of 1959. (USN via Harry Gann)

(Above) FJ-3M (139266) of VF-51 Screaming Eagles during carrier quals aboard ESSEX (CVA-9) in March of 1957. They deployed in July aboard BON HOMME RICHARD (CVA-31) with the FJ-3. (USN via Pete Bowers)

(Right) FJ-4B (141474) of VA-216 catching an arresting cable aboard LEXINGTON (CVA-16) in January of 1961. The cruise was to Laos, returning in June at which time LEXINGTON was redesignated as a CVS. (USN)

(Above) FJ-4B (141467) of VA-214 flying over Diamond Head, Hawaii during 1958 cruise aboard HORNET (CVA-12). VA-214 received the first Fleet FJ-4Bs in June of 1957. (USN)

(Right) FJ-4B (143528 and 143554) Furies of VA-146 in February of 1961 after returning from a WestPac cruise in December aboard the ORISKANY (CVA-34). (USN)

(Below) FJ-4B (143557) of VA-116 refueling FJ-4 (143529) of VA-146 in December of 1958 over Miramar. VA-116 replaced VA-144 which was transferred to CVW-5 and redesignated VA-52, and VA-116 became VA-144 in February of 1959 while deployed aboard RANGER (CVA-61). (USN)

F4D (F-6) SKYRAY - A month after service introduction of the Demon the Douglas F4D-1 (F-6A) Skyray entered Fleet service with the Be-Devilers of VF-74 and at the start of 1957 there were five Fleet squadrons operating the Skyray. The Skyray was the Navy's first delta wing fighter. Armament consisted of four 20MM cannons, and it could also carry six underwing pods with a total of forty 2.75-inch unguided rockets or four pods with seventy-six 2.75 rockets. Sidewinders were also available. In 1954 the Skyray established an official speed record, a first for a carrier based jet. The Skyray was an all-weather interceptor and was employed by eleven squadrons before being phased out by VF-13 during 1962.

(Above) F4D-1 (139088) Skyray of VF-213 Black Lions with Blue and White checkers which were used by the squadrons assigned to CVG-21. They deployed aboard LEXINGTON (CVA-16) in April of 1959 to WestPac. (USN via Bill Swisher)

(Above) F4D-1 (134959) of VF-102 Prowlers assigned to CVG-8 which was attached to the Fleets first super carrier FORRESTAL (CVA-59). They had just finished a shake down cruise in the Caribbean Sea during September of 1959. (Bill Swisher)

(Below) F4D-1 (134836) Skyray of VF-162 Hunters taxiing aboard INTREPID (CVA-11) during her last cruise as a CVA. The Hunters had replaced VF-74 also with Skyrays for this cruise. (Gordon Williams)

(Above) F4D-1 (134925) Skyray of VF-101 Grim Reapers and although assigned to ATG-201 the Reapers never deployed with ATG-201, they were instead replaced by VF-11 equipped with F2H-4 Demons for ATG-201's 1958 cruise. Master Field in January of 1958. (Bill Swisher)

(Below) F4D-1 (139058) of VF-51 Screaming Eagles just before deploying aboard TICONDEROGA (CVA-14) in March of 1960. (Bill Swisher)

VF-121
F3D-2T2 (124597) Skyknight of VF-121
NAS Miramar in 1958
197
NAVY
VF121
204
AM
1803
VF 21
NAVY
F11F-1 (141803) of VF-21
RANGER (CVA-61) in 1957
220
AF
1818
VF-33
NAVY
F11F-1 (141818) of VF-33
INTREPID (CVA-11) in 1957
105
109
NP
141873
NAVY
VF-211
F11F-1 (141873) of VF-211
LEXINGTON (CVA-16) in 1959
ASTRONAUTS
FIGHTING-33
VF-33
F11F-1 (141825) Tiger of VF-51
RANGER (CVA-61) in 1958
VA-156
NF
1825
105
NAVY
VF-51
101
NL
NAVY
VA156
F11F-1 (138634) of VA-156
HANCOCK (CVA-19) in 1958
105
NH
NAVY
VF156
F11F-1 (141738) of VA-156
SHANGRI-LA (CVA-38) in 1958
104
M
1773
NAVY
VF-191
F11F-1 (141773) of VF-191
BON HOMME RICHARD (CVA-31) in 1958/59
103
NJ
VF-121
NAVY
F11F-1 (141788) of VF-121
NAS Miramar in 1958
VA-116
F7U-3M (139917) Cutlass VA-116
HANCOCK (CVA-19) in 1957
NB
39917
NAVY
203
VA-116

F2H-3 (127590) of VF-71
RANDOLPH (CVA-15) in 1957

F2H-3 (127533) of VF-151
HANCOCK (CVA-19) in 1958

F2H (127683) of VF(AW)-4
NAS Quonset Point in 1959

F2H-4 (137598) Banshee of VF-11
ESSEX (CVA-9) in 1957

F2H-3 (126974) of VF-52
TICONDEROGA (CVA-14) in 1958

F2H-3 (126419) of VF-92
TICONDEROGA (CVA-14) in 1957

F2H-3 (126308) of VF-171
ROOSEVELT (CVA-42) in 1958

F2H-3 (126480) of VF-121
NAS Miramar in 1958

F2H-3 (137530) Banshee of VF-194
KEARSARGE (CVA-33) in 1957

F2H-2P (125683) of VFP-63
SARATOGA (CVA-60) in 1957

F2H-3 (126472) of VF-64
NAS Moffett Field in 1957

F2H-3 (127541) of VF-193
YORKTOWN (CVA-10) in 1957

F2H-3 (127519) of VA-152
BENNINGTON (CVA-20) in 1958

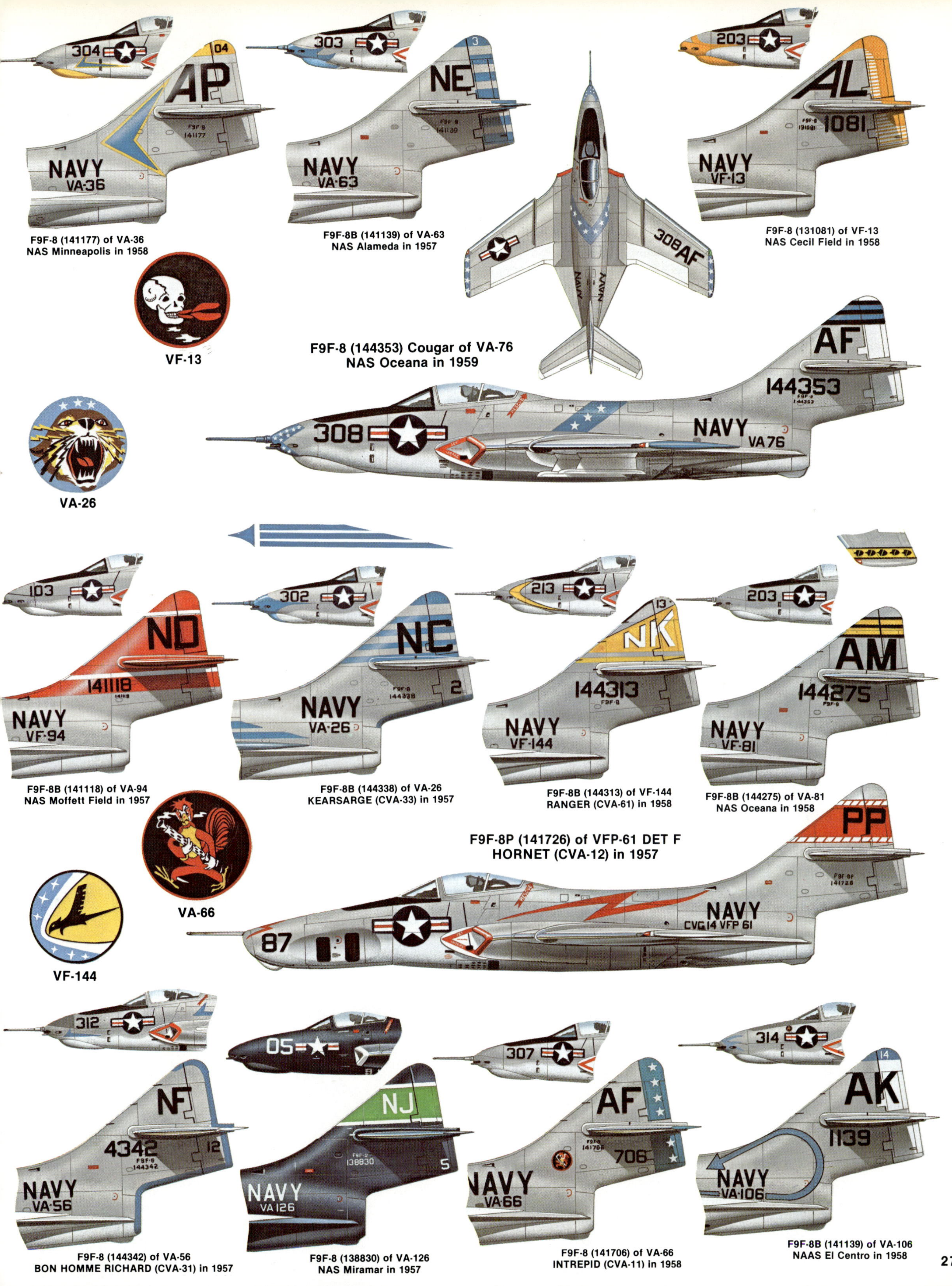

F9F-8 (141177) of VA-36
NAS Minneapolis in 1958

F9F-8B (141139) of VA-63
NAS Alameda in 1957

F9F-8 (144353) Cougar of VA-76
NAS Oceana in 1959

F9F-8 (131081) of VF-13
NAS Cecil Field in 1958

VF-13

VA-26

F9F-8B (141118) of VA-94
NAS Moffett Field in 1957

F9F-8B (144338) of VA-26
KEARSARGE (CVA-33) in 1957

F9F-8B (144313) of VF-144
RANGER (CVA-61) in 1958

F9F-8B (144275) of VA-81
NAS Oceana in 1958

F9F-8P (141726) of VFP-61 DET F
HORNET (CVA-12) in 1957

VA-66

VF-144

F9F-8 (144342) of VA-56
BON HOMME RICHARD (CVA-31) in 1957

F9F-8 (138830) of VA-126
NAS Miramar in 1957

F9F-8 (141706) of VA-66
INTREPID (CVA-11) in 1958

F9F-8B (141139) of VA-106
NAAS El Centro in 1958

F4D-1 (134959) of VF-102
RANDOLPH (CVA-15) in 1957

F4D-1 (134794) of VF-23
HORNET (CVA-12) in 1957

F4D-1 (134953) Skyray of VF-13
SHANGRI-LA (CVA-38) in 1960

F4D-1 (139200) of VMF(AW)-115
INDEPENDENCE (CVA-62) in 1963

F4D-1 (134795) of VF-162
INTREPID (CVA-11) in 1961

F4D-1 (134911) of VF-213
LEXINGTON (CVA-16) in 1958

F4D-1 (134809) of VF-141
RANGER (CVA-61) in 1958

F4D-1 (139072) of VMF(AW)-114
ROOSEVELT (CVA-42) in 1959

F4D-1 (134952) Skyray of VF-23
HANCOCK (CVA-12) in 1958

F4D-1 (134925) of VF-101
ESSEX (CVA-9) in 1958

F4D-1 (134868) of VF-74
ROOSEVELT (CVA-42) in 1957

F4D-1 (1434881) of VF-141
BON HOMME RICHARD (CVA-31) in 1957

F4D-1 (134772) of VFAW-3
NAS North Island in 1961

FJ-3M (136143) of VF-53
EARSARGE (CVA-33) in 1957/58

FJ-3M (136133) of VF-84
RANDOLPH (CVA-15) in 1958

FJ-3 (136072) of VF-62
ESSEX (CVA-9) in 1959/60

FJ-3 (135909) Fury of VF-91
TICONDEROGA (CVA-14) in 1958

FJ-3 (135928) of VF-154
HANCOCK (CVA-19) in 1958

FJ-3 (136073) of VF-73
RANDOLPH (CVA-15) in 1958

FJ-3 (135885) of GMGRU-1/CVG-11
SHANGRI-LA (CVA-38) in 1958

FJ-3 (139227) of VF-62
ESSEX (CVA-9) in 1958

FJ-3M (135990) Fury of CVG-5/VF-51
BON HOMME RICHARD (CVA-31) in 1957

FJ-3 (135912) of VF-121
NAS Miramar in 1958

FJ-3 (136087) of GMSRon-2
Chincoteague, Va in 1958

FJ-3M (141412) of VF-94
HORNET (CVA-12) in 1958

FJ-3 (141329) of VF-143
HANCOCK (CVA-19) in 1957

FJ-4B (145553) of VA-126
NAS Miramar in 1958

FJ-4B (141457) of VA-151
BENNINGTON (CVA-20) in 1958

FJ-4B (143556) of VA-192
BON HOMME RICHARD (CVA-31) in 1959

FJ-4B (143520) Fury of VA-116
HANCOCK (CVA-19) in 1958

FJ-4B (143571) of VA-63
MIDWAY (CVA-41) in 1958

FJ-4B (143503) of VA-146
RANGER (CVA-61) in 1958

FJ-4B (143527) of VA-214
HORNET (CVA-12) in 1958

FJ-4B (139548) of VFAW-3
NAS Moffett Field in 1958

A4D-2 (14918) Skyhawk of VA-81
FORRESTAL (CVA-59) in 1960

A4D-1 (142169) of VA-153
HANCOCK (CVA-19) in 1957

A4D-1 (142685) of VA-12
ROOSEVELT (CVA-42) in 1958

A4D-1 (139943) of VA-93
TICONDEROGA (CVA-14) in 1958

A4D-2 (142421) of VA-44
NAS Oceana in 1958

A4D-2 (142687) of VA-133
CONSTELLATION (CVA-62) in 1962

A4D-2N (148455) of CAG-6(VA-66)
ENTERPRISE (CVAN-63) in 1962

A4D-2 (144980) of VA-56
TICONDEROGA (CVA-14) in 1960

VA-133

A4D-2N (148456) Skyhawk of VA-72
INDEPENDENCE (CVA-62) in 1963

A4D-2 (144952) of VA-72
RANDOLPH (CVA-15) in 1959

A-4C (A4D-2N) (149951) of CVG-5/VA-55
TICONDEROGA (CVA-14) in 1963

A4D-2 (148495) of VA-36
SARATOGA (CVA-60) in 1962

A4D-2N (147741) of VA-46
ROOSEVELT (CVA-42) in 1961

VMA-324

VMA-225

A4B (A4D-2) (142520) Skyhawk of
VA-22, DET R to CVSG-53
KEARSARGE (CVS-33) in 1963

A4D-2 (142731) of VMA-225
ESSEX (CVA-9) in 1959

A-4E (A4D-5) (149661) of CAG-2 (VA-23)
MIDWAY (CVA-41) in 1963

A-4C (A4D-2) (143061) of VMA-324
INDEPENDENCE (CVA-62) in 1963

A-4C (A4D-2N) (150593) of VA-76
ENTERPRISE (CVAN-59) in 1963

AD-6 (139817) of VA-176
MCAS Yuma in 1958

AD-6 (137551) of VA-42
BENNINGTON (CVA-20) in 1957

AD-6 (137623) of VA-65
SHANGRI-LA (CVA-38) in 1957

VA-65

VA-42

AD-6 (139619) Skyraider of VA-65
INTREPID (CVA-11) in 1960

AD-6 (135337) of VA-196
TICONDEROGA (CVA-14) in 1958

AD-7 (142076) of VA-96
KEARSARGE (CVA-33) in 1957

AD-7 (142029) of VA-216
HORNET (CVA-12) in 1958

AD-6 (139701) of VA-145
HORNET (CVA-12) in 1957

VA-216

AD-6 (139758) Skyraider of VA-16
LAKE CHAMPLAIN (CVA-39) in 1957

VA(AW)-33

AD-5N (135043) of VA(AW)-33
INDEPENDENCE (CVA-62) in 1960

AD-5Q (132392) of VA-125
NAS Lemoore in 1962

AD-5N (132575) of VA(AW)-33
SARATOGA (CVA-60) in 1962

AD-5W (132743) of VAW-12
ESSEX (CVS-9) in 1960

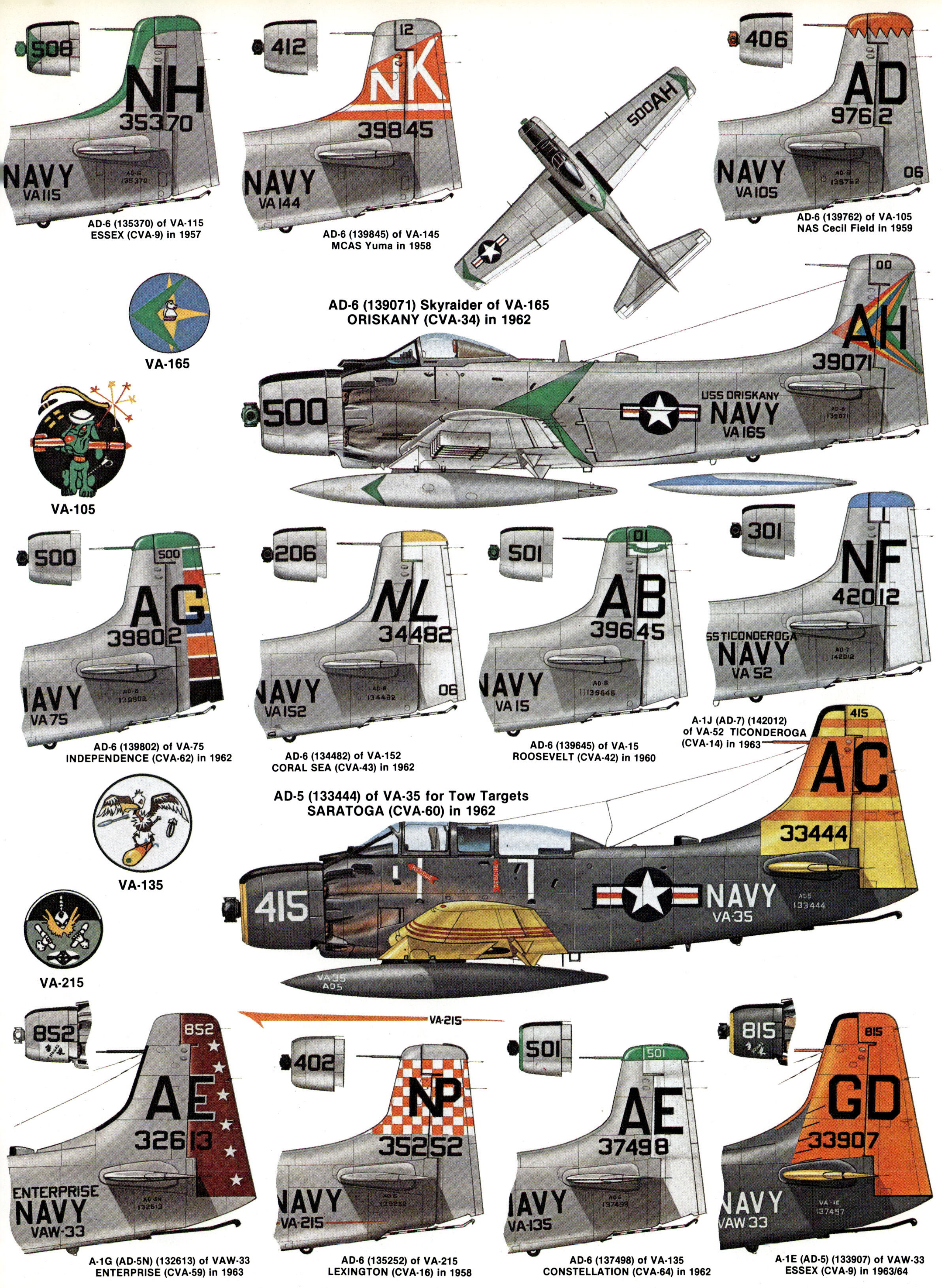

AD-6 (135370) of VA-115
ESSEX (CVA-9) in 1957

AD-6 (139845) of VA-145
MCAS Yuma in 1958

AD-6 (139762) of VA-105
NAS Cecil Field in 1959

AD-6 (139071) Skyraider of VA-165
ORISKANY (CVA-34) in 1962

VA-165

VA-105

AD-6 (139802) of VA-75
INDEPENDENCE (CVA-62) in 1962

AD-6 (134482) of VA-152
CORAL SEA (CVA-43) in 1962

AD-6 (139645) of VA-15
ROOSEVELT (CVA-42) in 1960

A-1J (AD-7) (142012)
of VA-52 TICONDEROGA
(CVA-14) in 1963

VA-135

AD-5 (133444) of VA-35 for Tow Targets
SARATOGA (CVA-60) in 1962

VA-215

A-1G (AD-5N) (132613) of VAW-33
ENTERPRISE (CVA-59) in 1963

AD-6 (135252) of VA-215
LEXINGTON (CVA-16) in 1958

AD-6 (137498) of VA-135
CONSTELLATION (CVA-64) in 1962

A-1E (AD-5) (133907) of VAW-33
ESSEX (CVA-9) in 1963/64

F3H-2M (137046) of VF-112
TICONDEROGA (CVA-14) in 1958

F3H-2 (143637) of VF-61
FORRESTAL (CVA-59) in 1959

F3H-2M (137072) of VF-24
LEXINGTON (CVA-16) in 1958

VF-41

VF-64

F3H-2 (143457) Demon of VF-64
MIDWAY (CVA-41) in 1958

F3H-2N (136973) of VF-114
SHANGRI-LA (CVA-38) in 1958

F3H-2 (143479) of VF-41
INDEPENDENCE (CVA-62) in 1959

F3H-2 (143437) of VF-41
NAS Oceana in 1958

BLACK ANGELS
VF-122

VF-122

USS INDEPENDENCE

F3H-2 (143576) of VF-14
ROOSEVELT (CVA-42) in 1962

VF-131

F3H-2 (143450) Demon of VF-31
SARATOGA (CVA-60) in 1960

USS CONSTELLATION

F3H-2N (137001) of VF-122
TICONDEROGA (CVA-14) in 1958

F3H-2 (143599) of VF-131
CONSTELLATION (CVA-64)
in 1962

F3H-2 (143446) of VF-193
BON HOMME RICHARD (CVA-31) in 1959

F3H-2 (133528) of VF-141
CONSTELLATION (CVA-64) in 1963

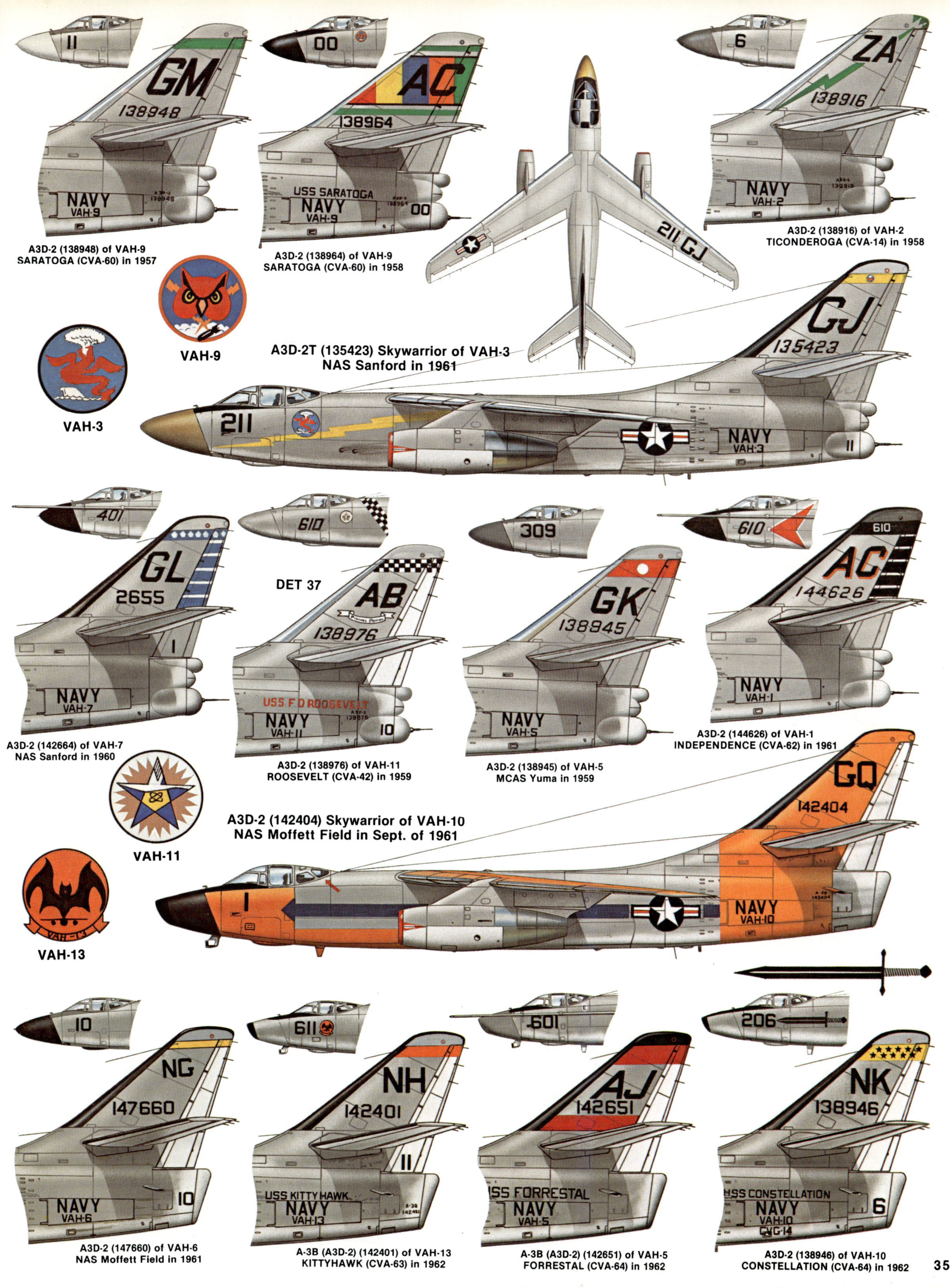

A3D-2 (138948) of VAH-9
SARATOGA (CVA-60) in 1957

A3D-2 (138964) of VAH-9
SARATOGA (CVA-60) in 1958

A3D-2 (138916) of VAH-2
TICONDEROGA (CVA-14) in 1958

VAH-9

VAH-3

A3D-2T (135423) Skywarrior of VAH-3
NAS Sanford in 1961

A3D-2 (142664) of VAH-7
NAS Sanford in 1960

DET 37

A3D-2 (138976) of VAH-11
ROOSEVELT (CVA-42) in 1959

A3D-2 (138945) of VAH-5
MCAS Yuma in 1959

A3D-2 (144626) of VAH-1
INDEPENDENCE (CVA-62) in 1961

VAH-11

VAH-13

A3D-2 (142404) Skywarrior of VAH-10
NAS Moffett Field in Sept. of 1961

A3D-2 (147660) of VAH-6
NAS Moffett Field in 1961

A-3B (A3D-2) (142401) of VAH-13
KITTYHAWK (CVA-63) in 1962

A-3B (A3D-2) (142651) of VAH-5
FORRESTAL (CVA-64) in 1962

A3D-2 (138946) of VAH-10
CONSTELLATION (CVA-64) in 1962

35

S2F-1 (133243) of VS-821
NAS New Orleans in 1962

S2F-2 (136707) of VS-28
WASP (CVS-18) in 1962

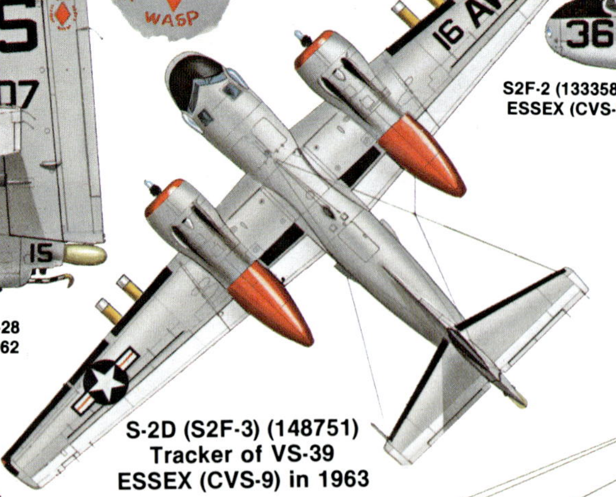

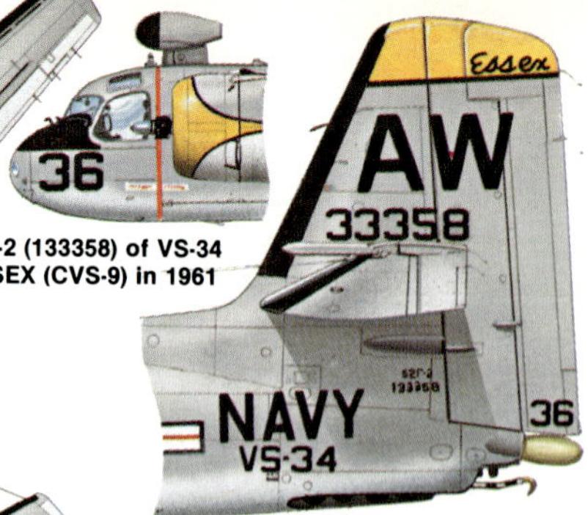

VS-751

VS-28

S2F-2 (133358) of VS-34
ESSEX (CVS-9) in 1961

S-2D (S2F-3) (148751)
Tracker of VS-39
ESSEX (CVS-9) in 1963

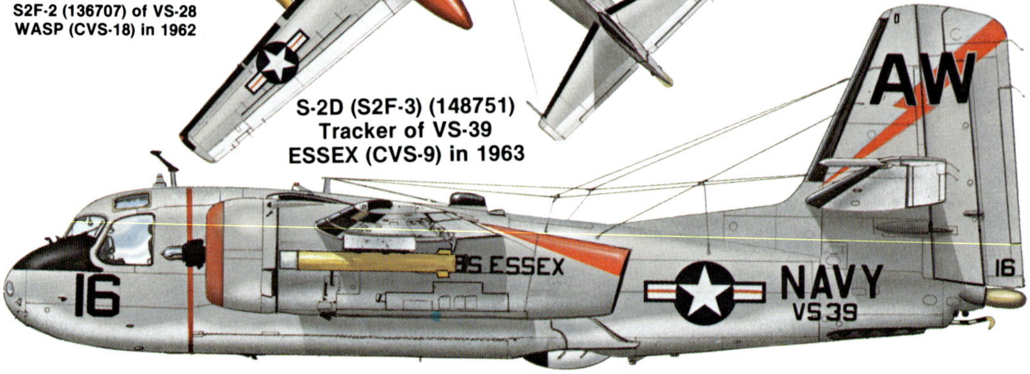

S2F-1 (133100) of VS-751
NAS Lakehurst in 1962

S2F-3 (147880) of VS-26
RANDOLPH (CVS-15) in 1962

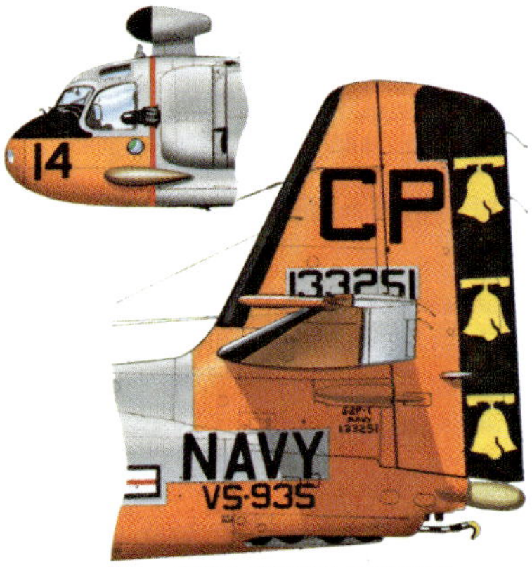

S2F-1 (133251) of VS-935
NAS Willow Grove in 1962

TF-1Q (136787) of VAW-11
NAS Alameda in 1962

VS-935

VS-24

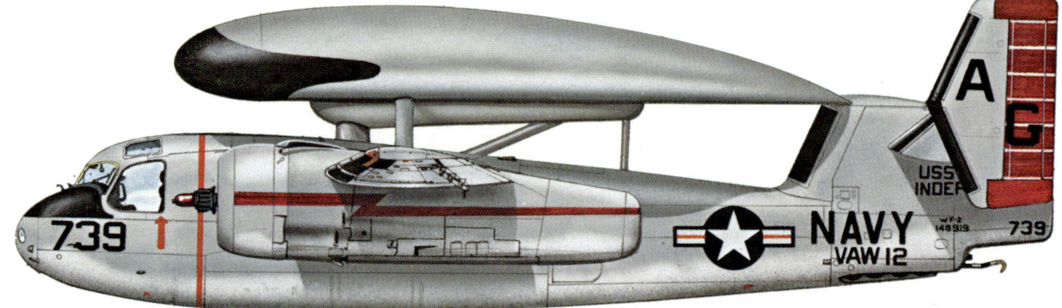

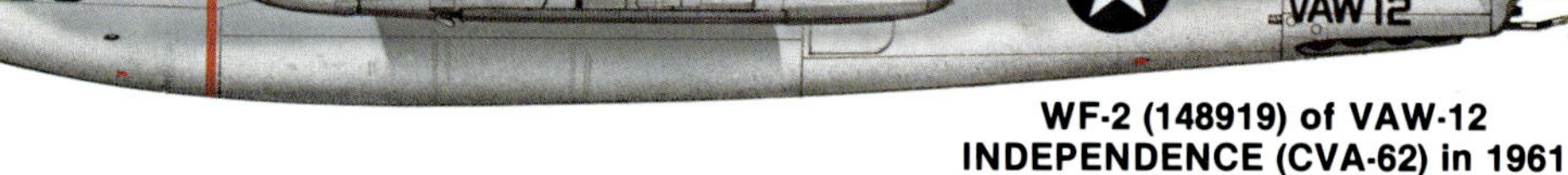

WF-2 (148919) of VAW-12
INDEPENDENCE (CVA-62) in 1961

S-2B (S2F-1S) (136709) of VS-24
INTREPID (CVS-11) in 1963

S2F-3 (148718) of VS-37
HORNET (CVS-12) in 1962

WF-2 (148137) of VAW-12
ROOSEVELT (CVA-42) in 1962

WF-2 (148125) of VAW-13, DET D
CORAL SEA (CVA-42) in 1960

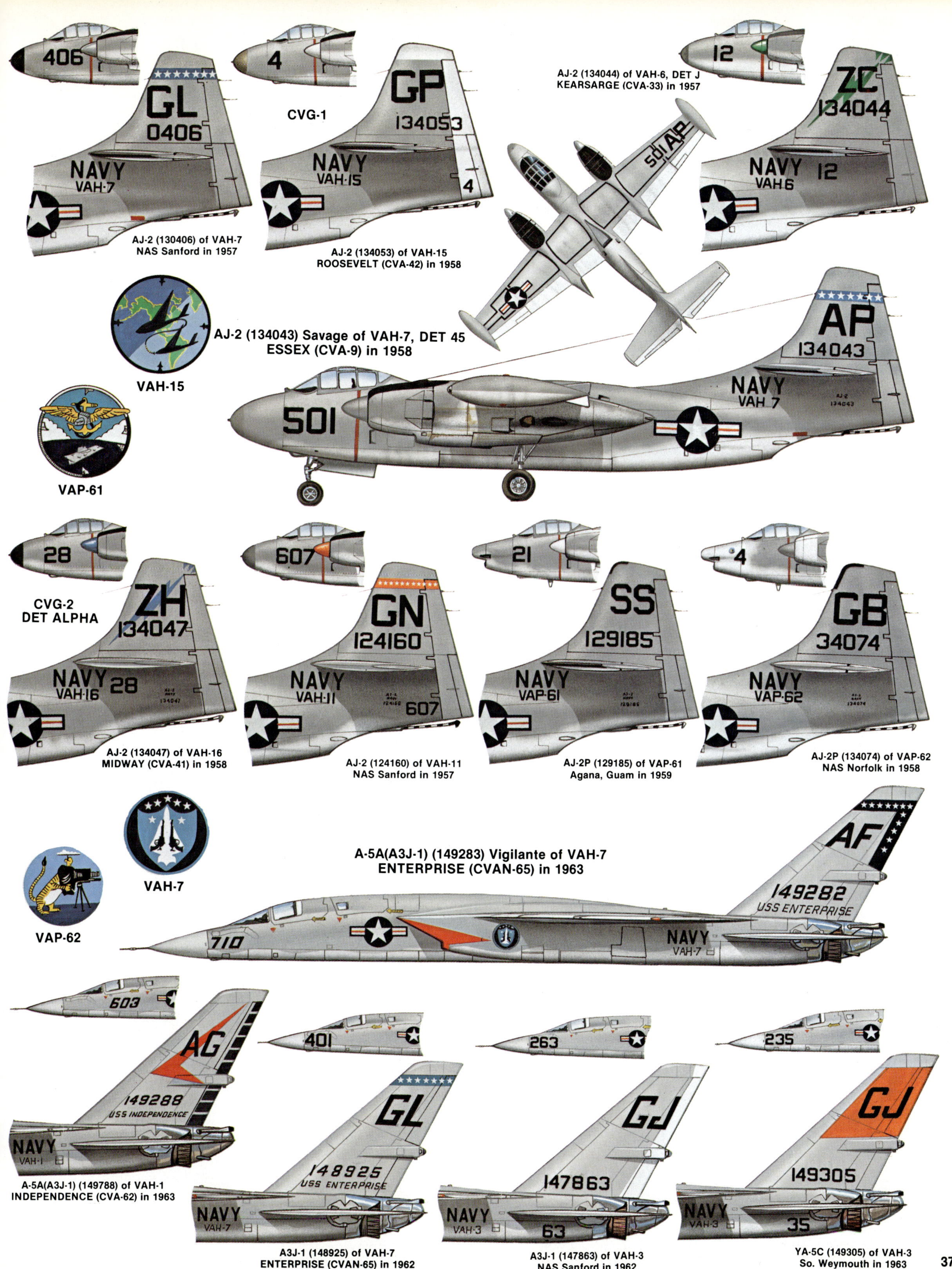

406
GL
0406
NAVY
VAH-7
AJ-2 (130406) of VAH-7
NAS Sanford in 1957

4
CVG-1
GP
134053
NAVY
VAH-15
AJ-2 (134053) of VAH-15
ROOSEVELT (CVA-42) in 1958

AJ-2 (134044) of VAH-6, DET J
KEARSARGE (CVA-33) in 1957

12
ZC
134044
NAVY
VAH-6

VAH-15
VAP-61

AJ-2 (134043) Savage of VAH-7, DET 45
ESSEX (CVA-9) in 1958

501
AP
134043
NAVY
VAH-7
AJ-2
134043

28
CVG-2
DET ALPHA
ZH
134047
NAVY
VAH-16
AJ-2 (134047) of VAH-16
MIDWAY (CVA-41) in 1958

607
GN
124160
NAVY
VAH-11
607
AJ-2 (124160) of VAH-11
NAS Sanford in 1957

21
SS
129185
NAVY
VAP-61
AJ-2P (129185) of VAP-61
Agana, Guam in 1959

4
GB
34074
NAVY
VAP-62
AJ-2P (134074) of VAP-62
NAS Norfolk in 1958

VAP-62
VAH-7

A-5A(A3J-1) (149283) Vigilante of VAH-7
ENTERPRISE (CVAN-65) in 1963

AF
149282
USS ENTERPRISE
710
NAVY
VAH-7

603
AG
149288
USS INDEPENDENCE
NAVY
VAH-1
A-5A(A3J-1) (149788) of VAH-1
INDEPENDENCE (CVA-62) in 1963

401
GL
148925
USS ENTERPRISE
NAVY
VAH-7
A3J-1 (148925) of VAH-7
ENTERPRISE (CVAN-65) in 1962

263
GJ
147863
NAVY
VAH-3
63
A3J-1 (147863) of VAH-3
NAS Sanford in 1962

235
GJ
149305
NAVY
VAH-3
35
YA-5C (149305) of VAH-3
So. Weymouth in 1963

F8U-1 (144461) of VF-211
MIDWAY (CVA-41) in 1958

F8U-1 (143744) of VF-142
NAS Miramar in 1957

F8U-1 (146932) of VF-103
FORRESTAL (CVA-59) in 1958

F8U-1 (135347) Crusader of VF-11
ROOSEVELT (CVA-42) in 1961

F8U-1 (143742) of VF-32
SARATOGA (CVA-60) in 1958

F8U-1E (145417) of VF-174
INDEPENDENCE (CVA-62) in 1961

F8U-1 (145399) of VF-124
NAS Moffett Field in 1960

F8U-1 (145389) of VF-91
RANGER (CVA-61) in 1959

F8U-1 (146934) Crusader of VF-84
INDEPENDENCE (CVA-62) in 1961

F8U-1E (145375) of VF-62
ENTERPRISE (CVAN-65) in 1962

F8U-2NE (149180) of VF-141
CONSTELLATION (CVA-64) in 1962

F8U-1E (145460) of VMF-251
SHANGRI-LA (CVA-38) in 1962

F8U-2N (148649) of VF-154
CORAL SEA (CVA-43) in 1963

F8U-1 (144436) of VF-211
HANCOCK (CVA-19) in 1962

F-8A (F8U-1) (145359) of VF-191
BON HOMME RICHARD (CVA-31) in 1963

F-8A (F8U-1) (143752) of VF-162
ORISKANY (CVA-34) in 1963

VF-162

VFP-62

RF-8A (F8U-1P) (146889) Crusader of VFP-62
ENTERPRISE (CVAN-65) in 1963

F8U-2 (145595) of VMF-323
(CVG-14) LEXINGTON (CVA-16) in 1961/62

F8U-1P (146878) of VFP-63, DET-G
ORISKANY (CVA-34) in 1962

F8U-1P (146862) of VFP-62
INDEPENDENCE (CVA-62) in 1962

F8U-1 (143707) of VF-124
San Francisco in 1958

VF-114

VMF-323

F4H-1 (143631) Phantom of VF-74
FORRESTAL (CVA-59) in 1962

F4H-1 (148422) of VF-121
NAS Miramar in 1961

F4H-1 (148405) of VF-114
KITTYHAWK (CVA-63) in 1962

F-4B (F4H-1) (148393) of VF-102
ENTERPRISE (CVAN-65) in 1962

F-4B (F4H-1) (149410) of VF-96
RANGER (CVA-61) in 1963

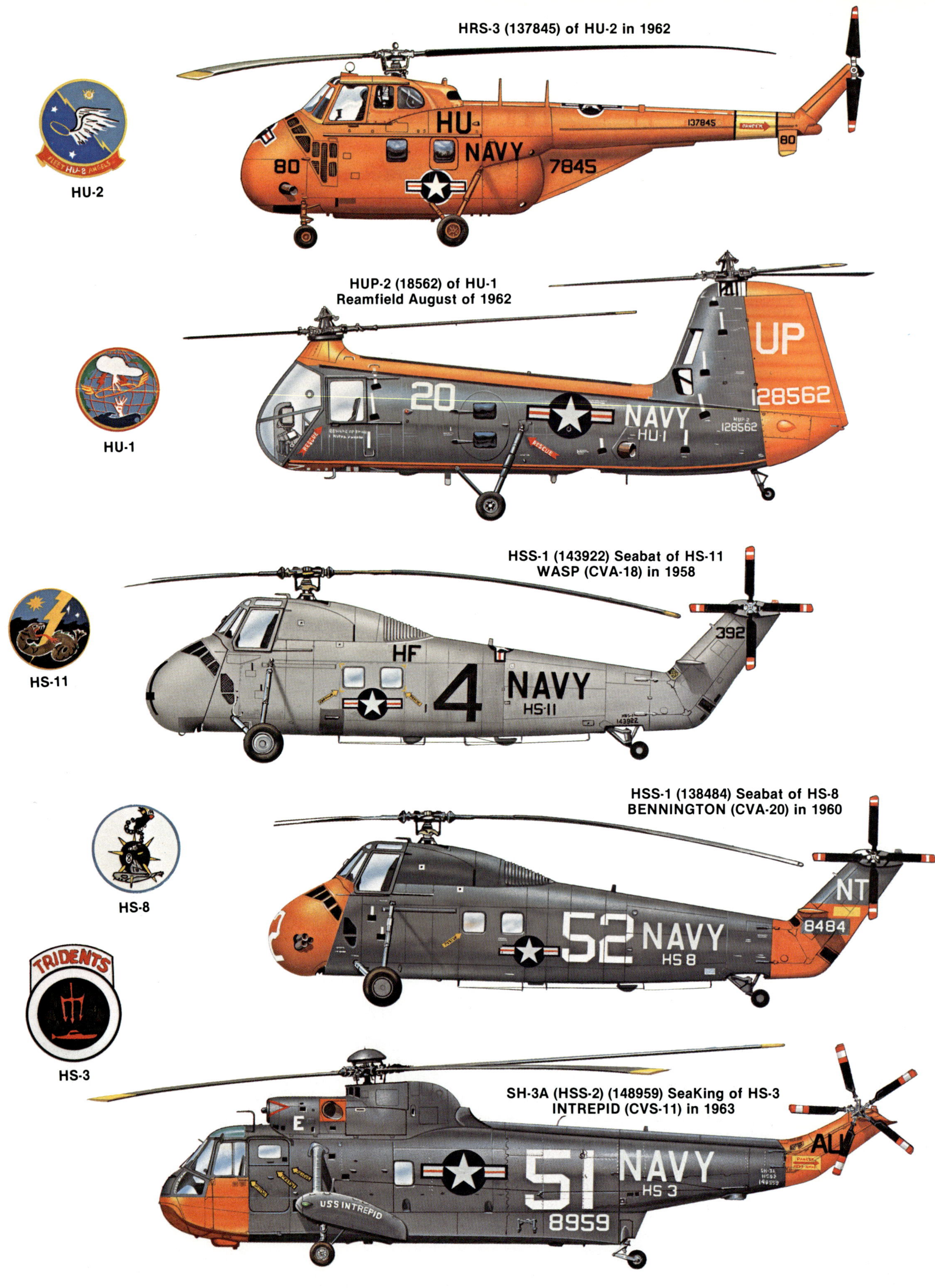

HRS-3 (137845) of HU-2 in 1962
HU-2
HUP-2 (18562) of HU-1
Reamfield August of 1962
HU-1
HSS-1 (143922) Seabat of HS-11
WASP (CVA-18) in 1958
HS-11
HSS-1 (138484) Seabat of HS-8
BENNINGTON (CVA-20) in 1960
HS-8
TRIDENTS
HS-3
SH-3A (HSS-2) (148959) SeaKing of HS-3
INTREPID (CVS-11) in 1963

F11F (F-11) TIGER - The Grumman F11F-1 Tiger entered Fleet service first with attack squadron VA-156 in March of 1957. When VA-156 was transferred to CVG-11 the Squadron was redesignated VF-111. The Tiger reached a peak of five squadrons. The F11F introduced area-rule but suffered from limited range and was over shadowed by newer types. The last squadrons to operate the Tiger was the Astronauts of VF-33 and the Sundowners of VF-111 in 1961.

(Right) F11F-1 Tigers of VF-51 Screaming Eagles in June of 1958 during their transition to the Tiger. The squadron trim color is Red with the Eagle on a Red chevron on the nose just in front of the aircraft squadron. VF-51 never deployed with the Tiger since they transitioned to the F4D-1 Skyray a short time later. (USN via Jim Sullivan)

(Above) F11F-1 (141785), one of VF-191's newly acquired Tigers at Moffett Field in May of 1958. They had converted from the FJ-3 Fury in late 1957 and were scheduled to deploy aboard BON HOMME RICHARD (CVA-31) in October. (Bill Larkins)

(Below) F11F-1 (141820) of VF-111 Sundowners at Miramar in June of 1960. They transitioned to the F8U-2N Crusader shortly after this. VF-111 had been previously designated VA-156. (Bill Swisher)

(Above) F11F-1 Tiger (141849) of VF-211 moving forward after landing aboard LEXINGTON (CVA-16) in May of 1959. (USN)

(Below) F11F-1 (138636) of VA-156 at Moffett Field in June of 1957. They deployed aboard HANCOCK (CVA-19) the following year in February. (Bill Larkins via Clay Jansson)

F3H (F-3) DEMON - The McDonnell all-weather F3H-2N Demon had been introduced by the Tophatters of VF-14 in March of 1956. The F3H-2M (MF-3B) followed and was equipped with the Sparrow III missile for interceptor duties while the F3H-2 (F-3B) combined the features of the -2N and -2M, by carrying four advance Sparrow III missiles and four 20MM cannons. VF-64 fired the first Sparrow IIIs outside the Continental United States (CONUS) while aboard MIDWAY. The Demon was able to refuel other aircraft through the use of the buddy system which was a 300 gallon tank with hose. A total of twenty-one Fleet squadrons operated the Demon at its peak and by the end of 1963 the total was at four.

(Right) F-3B (F3H-2) (136976) of VF-161 Chargers just back from a cruise aboard ORISKANY (CVA-38) in December of 1962. All trim markings are in Red. Miramar in January of 1963. (Harry Gann)

(Above) F3H-2M (137056) Fury of VF-112 at Miramar in August of 1957 with Red trim colors. VA-112 was re-assigned from CVG-11 to ATG-1 (NA tail Code) and assigned 100 series nose numbers. (Clay Jansson)

(Below) F3H-2N (136973) of VF-114 Executioners at Miramar in August of 1957. VF-114 was the second Demon squadron assigned to CVG-11 at this time. (Larry Smalley)

(Above) F3H-2N (137041) of VF-112 at Oakland Airport in September of 1958 prior to a cruise aboard TICONDEROGA (CVA-14) in October with ATG-1 to WestPac. Prior to this they had been assigned to CVG-11. (Larry Smalley)

(Below) F3H-2 (143435) of VF-21 Freelancers entangled in the barrier after its tailhook failed to lower during landing aboard MIDWAY (CVA-41) in April. They had been at sea only three weeks when this accident occurred. (USN)

(Above) F3H-2 (143440) of VF-193 Ghost Riders in Blue trim with thin White outlines and CVG-19 tail code. VF-193 deployed to WestPac in July of 1962 aboard BON HOMME RICHARD (CVA-31). (Larry Smalley)

(Below) F3H-2M (137088) of VF-24 Corsairs at Oakland in September of 1957. The squadron was assigned to CVG-21 shortly after this for a deployment aboard LEXINGTON (CVA-16) in 1958. VF-24 was re-designated to VF-211 in March of 1958 to align their designator with CVG-21. (Bill Larkins)

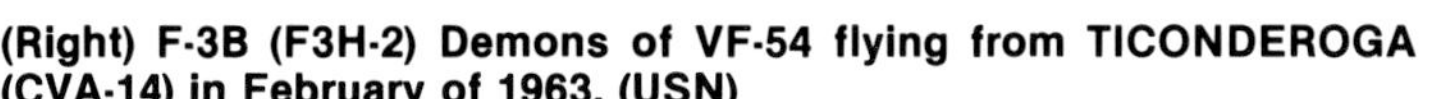

(Above) F3H-2 (143442) of VF-92 Silver Kings at San Francisco Airport in September of 1960. (Larry Smalley)

(Right) F-3B (F3H-2) Demons of VF-54 flying from TICONDEROGA (CVA-14) in February of 1963. (USN)

(Below) F3H-2 (133489) of VF-31 Felix being hoisted aboard SARATOGA (CVA-60) in May of 1959, prior to a deployment to the Med. Crusaders of VF-32, VF-31's sister squadron are already on-board. (USN)

A4D (A-4) SKYHAWK - The Douglas A4D-1 Skyhawk was another type that had entered the Fleet in 1956 and at the start of 1957 there were only two Fleet squadrons, VA-72 and VA-93. The A4D-1 had the capability for nuclear or conventional weapons but required highly trained pilots since few electronics were carried. For a mission requiring navigation and bomb aiming an electronics pod was carried. The up graded A4D-2 (A-4B) with provisions for inflight refueling went into service with VA-12 in February of 1958 and began to replace the attack fighter-bomber versions of the Fury and Cougar. The A4D-2N (A-4C) was a limited all-weather night attack version with a nose 9 inches longer, entering the Fleet with the Golden Dragons of VA-192 in July of 1959. The A4D-5 (A-4E) incorporated a new engine and two addi- tional wing stations which permitted the Skyhawk to carry 8200 pounds of ordnance. The A-4E entered the Fleet with the Black Knights of VA-23 in late 1962.

(Above) A4D-1 (142169) Skyhawk of VA-153 Blue Tail Flies at Moffett Field in May of 1958, just prior to their deployment aboard HANCOCK (CVA-19). (Larry Smalley)

(Left) A4D-2 (144885) of VA-34 Blue Blasters in Blue trim. They are conducting carrier quals aboard ESSEX (CVS-9) during April of 1961. Later they deployed aboard SARATOGA (CVA-60) for a Med cruise in November. (USN)

(Above) A-4B (A4D-2) (144907) of VA-164 Ghostriders loaded with MK-81 bombs somewhere in the Pacific. The Ghostriders had deployed in August of 1963 from CONUS. (USN)

(Left) A4D-2 (145003) of VA-83 Rampagers while in the Med flying from FORRESTAL (CVA-59) in April of 1960. Eight diamonds are carried on the rudder denoting CVG-8. (USN via Pete Bowers)

(Below) A4D-1s of VA-93 Blue Blazers flying by Mount Fuji during their 1957/58 cruise aboard TICONDEROGA (CVA-14). VF-91, VA-122 and VA-95 used the same CVG-9 markings. (USN via Harry Gann)

(Above) A-4B (A4D-2) (142830) of VA-22, DET-R attached to CVSG-53 providing CAP for KEARSARGE (CVS-33). This Skyhawk carries sidewinder missile rails while deployed as part of a four aircraft DET aboard KEARSARGE during the fall of 1963. (Toda Koda)

(Right) A-4C (A4D-2N) (149638) of VA-86 Sidewinders painted in Orange to match the squadron nose numbers and trim color. They deployed to the Med in August of 1963, returning in March the following year. (Roger Besecker)

(Above) A-4C (A4D-2N) (150593) of VA-76 nicknamed the "Spirits of '76" at the 1963 Paris Air Show. There were two other Skyhawk squadrons attached to CVG-6 for this cruise, VA-64 and VA-66. (Larry Smalley Collection)

(Right) A-4C (A4D-2N) (148445) of VA-46 Clansman aboard SHANGRI LA (CVA-38) in the Med having deployed in October of 1963. (Duane Kasulka Collection)

(Below) A4D-2 (142708) of VA-72 Blue Hawks being readied for launch from RANDOLPH (CVA-15) in December of 1958. (USN)

F8U (F-8) CRUSADER - The Chance Vought F8U-1 Crusader went into Fleet service with VF-32 of the Atlantic Fleet and VF-154 of the Pacific Fleet in March of 1957. The F-8A was armed with four 20MM cannons and provisions for two Sidewinder missiles. A rocket pod which opened from the bottom of the fuselage fired thirty-two 2.75-inch unguided rockets, however, this provision was quickly eliminated. To achieve improved carrier landing characteristics, the wing was pivoted seven degrees which permitted maximum visibility during landing and takeoff. It was followed by the F8U-1E (F-8B) a limited all-weather interceptor with two additional Sidewinders on the fuselage. Next was the F8U-2 (F-8C) which was distinguishable by the addition of two ventral fins under the tail section. The Jolly Rogers of VF-84 introduced the F-8C in 1959. The F8U-2N (F-8D), a further upgrading of the Crusader, entered Fleet service the following year at which time a total of ten squadrons were operating the Crusader. The F8U-2NE (F-8E) was introduced to the Fleet in 1963 and incorporated improved radar for all-weather capability and removable under wing bomb racks for the ground attack role. Total Fleet fighter squadrons equipped with the Crusader at the end of 1963 was fifteen, with the majority being equipped with the F-8E.

(Above) F8U-1 (145389) Crusaders of VF-91 Red Lightings at Miramar in 1960. The Red Lightings previously flew the FJ-3 Fury. (Pete Bowers via Lional Paul)

(Above) F8U-1 (143810) of VF-62 Boomerangs with afterburner lit launches from ENTERPRISE (CVAN-65) as part of an air power demonstration for President Kennedy in April of 1962. (USN)

(Left) F8U-1 (143788) of VF-174 Hell's Razors at Miami in May of 1958 just prior to becoming a RAG training squadron for LANT Fleet Crusaders. They would be assigned to RCVG-4 in their new training role. (Bill Swisher)

(Below) F8U-1 (145517) of VF-33 aboard INTREPID (CVA-11) during carrier quals in April of 1961 prior to actual deployment in August. Their previous aircraft had been the F11F-1 Tiger. (Clay Jansson Collection)

(Above) F8U-1 (143707) of VF-124 Stingers at the San Francisco Airport during May of 1958. VF-124 was disestablished in April and never actually deployed with CVG-15. At this same time VF-53 became VF-124 as part of the new RCVG-12. (Larry Smalley)

(Right) F8U-2NE (149180) of VF-141 Iron Angels at Miramar in 1962. The squadron had converted from the F3H Demon after returning from their last cruise aboard LEXINGTON (CVA-16) in May. (Harry Gann)

(Below) F-8D (F8U-2) (148710) of VF-32 Swordsmen on display at the Paris air show in 1963. CVG-3 had deployed in March for the Med and returned in October to CONUS. (Lional Paul Collection)

(Right) F-8A (F8U-1) (143752) of VF-162 Hunters at Miramar in January of 1963. They deployed aboard ORISKANY (CVA-34) in August to the Western Pacific. (Clay Jansson)

(Below) F-8C (F8U-2) (146991) of VF-24 at Miramar having just returned from a cruise aboard MIDWAY (CVA-41) in October of 1962. During their next deployment VF-24 received 400 series aircraft nose numbers to align with the squadron designator. (Clay Jansson)

F4H (F-4) PHANTOM II - The McDonnell F4H-1F (F-4A) arrived at the newly designated replacement training squadrons VF-121 for the Pacific Fleet and VF-101 in the Atlantic Fleet during December of 1961. The first Fleet carrier squadron was VF-74 in July of 1961 which deployed to the Mediterranean in August of the following year with F4H-1s (F-4Bs). The F-4B had a new radome shape, re-designed canopy, boundary layer control, and a different engine. Some F-4As were brought up to B standards and redesignated. The Aardvarks of VF-114 of the Pacific Fleet deployed two months later to WestPac. The Phantom II was the Navy's first truly all-weather carrier fighter and began replacing the F-3 Demon and by the end of 1963 there were ten Phantom II fleet squadrons, and only four Demon squadrons. The Phantom II was also the first Navy fighter to be built without guns, its armament being missiles. The remaining fighter squadrons operated the F-8 Crusader aboard ESSEX class carriers.

(Right) F4H-1 (148402) Phantom II of VF-102 Diamond Backs being brought up to the ENTERPRISE (CVAN-65) flight deck during her first cruise in 1962. (USN via Fred Harl)

(Above) F-4B (F4H-1) (151438) of VF-96 Fighting Falcons after having returned from a cruise aboard RANGER (CVA-61) in June of 1963. Few fighter squadrons used a 600 series nose number. (Duane Kasulka)

(Below) F-4B (F4H-1) (149417) of VF-14 Top Hatters converted from the F3H Demon after their ROOSEVELT (CVA-42) cruise in April of 1963. They deployed in April of the following year aboard ROOSEVELT for its 15th Med cruise. (Duane Kasulka Collection)

(Above) F4H-1 (148391) of VF-114 Executioners at North Island in August of 1962 just prior to their first cruise. They deployed aboard KITTYHAWK (CVA-63) from September of 1962 through April of 1963. (Bill Swisher)

(Below) F4H-1 (149433) Phantom II of VF-41 Black Spades after their first cruise aboard INDEPENDENCE (CVA-62) in 1962. The spade is Black and the diagonal fuselage band is Red. (Duane Kasulka Collection)

HEAVY ATTACK

At at the beginning of 1957 heavy attack squadrons were primarily equipped with the North American AJ Savage plus a few of the new Douglas A3D-1 Skywarriors which had been introduced into Fleet service the year before by VAH-1. With the pending arrival in 1955 of the new Skywarrior the Navy established five heavy attack squadrons (VAHs) and redesignated those composite squadrons in the heavy attack role to VAH squadrons the following year. To facilitate transitional training from the propeller driven Savage to the jet powered Skywarrior the Navy established the Heavy Attack Training Unit, Pacific (HATUPAC) at San Diego in early 1957, which later moved to Whidbey Island, and was redesignated VAH-123 as part of RCVG-12 in June of 1957. The A3D-2 had a weapon bay change permitting a wider variety of external stores including a refueling pack to be carried. The first A-3B entered the Fleet with VAH-2 in 1957, and by 1958 the Skywarrior had replaced the Savage except for those aircraft modified to the aerial refueling role. Aerial refueling was considered so crucial to the Navy that two new squadrons, VAH-15 and VAH-16 were established on 15 January 1958 solely as refueling squadrons on Savage tankers. The advantage of aerial refueling were many; increased range, aircraft losing fuel could be nursed back to a carrier, Combat Air Patrols could be on station longer, and returning aircraft could loiter longer if a carrier deck was clogged.

The first A3D Skywarrior tanker arrived in 1959, and as the new tanker became available Savage tankers were phased out by disestablishing those squadrons equipped with the Savage. The last twenty-one A3D-2s, delivered between April of 1960 and January of 1961, had a cambered wing leading edge, inflight refueling capability, a new bombing system, and the tail turret replaced with ECM avionics. These modifications were later retro-fitted to most of the earlier A3Ds. During 1961 the Navy added two more VAH squadrons with the establishment of VAH-13 in January and VAH-10 in May providing dedicated VAH squadrons for those CVGs operating from the larger carriers. These refueling squadrons were normally equipped with twelve aircraft and deployed seven to ten aircraft aboard the larger carriers and four plane DETs aboard the smaller ESSEX class carriers.

The fastest and only supersonic Navy bomber was the North American A3J-1 (A-5A) Vigilante which was designed to take full advantage of the new super-carriers. The Vigilante was a Mach 2, two place attack bomber capable of carrying nuclear ordnance. The Vigilante also could carry two underwing pylons for 400 gallon fuel tanks or additional weaponry. The first A3J-1 Vigilante was received in June of 1961 by RAG squadron VAH-3 which began the Fleet Introduction Program (FIP) for the first Fleet squadron, the Peacemakers of VAH-7, which began transitioning in August and received their first A3J-1 Vigilantes in January of 1962. The following year VAH-1 received the A3J-1 and deployed aboard the new ENTERPRISE six months later. By the end of 1961 the Navy had two Fleet Vigilante squadrons and ten Skywarrior squadrons. When shored based they often employed the TV-2 and F9F-8B (AF-9J) as support aircraft.

(Above) AJ-2 (134046) of VAH-6, DET-F attached to CVG-14 flying from HORNET (CVA-12) during 1957. (USN)

(Above) AJ-2 (134042) Savage of VAH-16 off the coast of Japan in 1959. This Savage established a record of 104 hook-ups in one hour. VAH-16 was one of two squadrons especially established as an aerial refueling squadron. The F9F-8P (144393) is from Marine Photo-Composite Squadron 3 (VMCJ-3). (Clay Jansson)

(Above) AJ-2 (124162) Savage of VAH-11 in storage at Litchfield Park in March of 1960, the fate of the now obsolete Savage. Few Savages carried CVG tail codes since most served in DETs. (Bill Swisher)

(Below) AJ-2 (134043) Savage of VAH-7 DET-45 refueling an FJ-3M (139232) Fury of VF-62 while deployed aboard ESSEX (CVA-9) in June of 1958. They had deployed in February and did not return to CONUS until November. (USN)

(Above) A3D-2 (138932) Skywarrior of VAH-1 Tigers using JATO bottles for takeoff in May of 1961. The Tigers provided in-flight refueling for Project LANA, the Bendix Trophy world speed record flown by an F4H Phantom II. (MDAC via Fred Harl)

(Below) A3D-2 (142650) of VAH-9 with Green tail trim colors refueling an F4H-1 (148261), DET-A during a training exercise in 1962. (MDAC via Fred Harl)

(Below) A3D-2 (142236) of VAH-6, DET-L in typical West Coast identification scheme for DETs by using their own tail code and a 1 through 99 nose numbering system for aircraft identification. (USN)

(Left) A3D-2 (138974) of VAH-5 Savage Sons carrying a squadron tail code and 300 series nose numbers. Squadron trim colors are Red, the nose numbers were based on the parent shore based command and normally changed to a 600 series when deployed with a CVG. (Clay Jansson Collection)

(Below) A3D-2 (142664) of VAH-7 Go-Devils at Yuma in December of 1959. Trim colors are Blue with a 400 series nose number. These numbers were used between cruises and were aligned by the squadron within the shore based command. (Bill Swisher)

(Above) A-3B (A3D-2) (142401) of VAH-13 Bats attached to CVG-11 which was deployed from KITTYHAWK (CVA-63). Whidley Island in April of 1963. (Doug Olson via Clay Jansson)

(Below) A-5A (A3J-1) (149288) Vigilante of VAH-1, they received their first Vigilante in January of 1963 at Sanford. By August they were deployed aboard INDEPENDENCE (CVA-62) to the Med. (Pete Bowers)

(Right) A3D-2 (138937) of VAH-5 aboard ENTERPRISE (CVAN-65) in April of 1962. They deployed aboard FORRESTAL (CVA-59) in August to the Med. Trim color is Red. (USN)

(Below) A3D-2 (138955) of VAH-10 with a 200 nose number series during CONSTELLATION's (CVA-64) second cruise in 1963. The 200 series nose numbers resulted from VA-146 using the 600 series as VF-142 was not attached to GVG-14. (USN)

CARRIER HEAVY ATTACK

VAH-1	GH	VAH-6	ZC	VAH-11	GN
VAH-2	ZA	VAH-7	GL	VAH-13	GP
VAH-3	GJ	VAH-8	ZD	VAH-15	GR
VAH-4	ZB	VAH-9	GM	VAH-16	ZH
VAH-5	GK	VAH-10	ZR	VAH-123	NJ *

RCVG-12 Tail code. VAH-15 and VAH-16 were decommissioned 1960. The usage of VAH squadron tail codes was straight forward until 1959 when the Atlantic Fleet began using the parent CVG tail codes. This resulted in part from the decision in April of 1958 to assign a VAH squadron or DET to each CVG as were the VF and VA squadrons. A 600 series of aircraft nose numbers was adopted in December for these VAH squadrons.

(Below) A-5A (A3J-1) Vigilante of VAH-7 Peacemakers aboard ENTERPRISE (CVAN-65) in February of 1963. CVG-6 switched from 'AF' to 'AE' tailcodes shortly after this, deploying in February on ENTERPRISE's second cruise. (USN)

SPECIAL PURPOSE CARRIER SQUADRONS

Attached to each CVG/ATG were a variety of special purpose Detachments (DETs) with two to five aircraft deployed from a parent squadron. These special purpose squadrons supplied DETs to multiple carriers, often deploying three to four DETs at one time. These squadron DETs included: photo-reconnaissance (both fighter [Light] and attack [Heavy]), airborne early-warning, and a Helicopter DET for utility duties. Fighter and attack all-weather DETs where gradually phased out since the new jet powered attack and fighter aircraft entering the Fleet had all-weather capability.

CARRIER ALL-WEATHER FIGHTER

The variety of aircraft types employed by VF(AW)-3 had been reduced to the FJ-3M (MF-1C) Fury, F8U-1 (F-8A) Crusader, F3H-2N (F-3C) Demon and the F4D-1 (F-6A) Skyray. VF(AW)-4 continued to operate the McDonnell F2H-2N and F2H-3 Banshee plus the AD-5 Skyraider and a few TVs and an SNB-5 until disestablished in 1963.

The Demon was phased out in favor of the Skyray by VF(AW)-3 and was their primary aircraft type when disestablished on 2 May 1958. Their duties were taken over by VF-124, now a replacement training squadron. Considerable confusion resulted when an element of Fleet All Weather Training Unit Pacific (FAWTUPAC) was designated VF(AW)-3 with their own tail code of 'PA', and given squadron status the same day that old VF(AW)-3 was disestablished. The new VF(AW)-3 supplied Skyrays for Continental Air Defense Command under USAF control and remained in that role until disestablished in March of 1963.

The carrier all-weather fighter role was now exclusively performed by fighter squadrons operating the Demon, Crusader and Phantom II.

Prior to this the two squadrons operated the Douglas AD-5N (A-1G) Skyraider, the newly delivered Grumman TF-1Q (EC-1A), and several Beech SNB-5s (TC-45Js) for utility and training duties. The TF-1Q was the first naval aircraft equipped for electronic jamming with VA(AW)-35 receiving the first one in January of 1957. Later the same year AD-5Q (EA-1F) Skyraiders were added and began deploying in three and four plane DETs. VA(AW)-33 added a Grumman S2F-1 (S-2A) Tracker in 1958 for utility duties. VA(AW)-35 added the AD-5, AD-6 and AD-7 (A-1E, A-1H and A-1J) the same year and ten North American T-28Bs in 1959. VA(AW)-35 was deployed with the AD-5N and AD-5Q but this was cut short when they were disestablished that same year. With the disestablishing of VA(AW)-35 and the redesignation of the Knighthawks to VAW-33 the dedicated squadron role of carrier all-weather attack was passed to conventional carrier attack squadrons equipped with all-weather attack aircraft.

CARRIER ALL-WEATHER FIGHTER

VF(AW)-3 TT (Decom 1958)	VF(AW)-4 GC (Decom 1962)
FAWTUPAC/VF(AW)-3 PA (Decom 1963)	

(Above) F2H-4 (127580) of VF(AW)-4 at Quonset Point in January of 1959. They also operated several TV-2s for utility duties. (USN)

(Below) F8U-1 (142409) Crusader of VF(AW)-3 at Moffett Field in May of 1957. The squadron was de-established in May of 1958. (Bill Larkins)

(Above) F4D-1 (139162) Skyray of VF(AW)-3 Blue Nemesis, the second squadron to carry this designation. VF(AW)-3 operated in support of Continental Air Defense Command. North Island August of 1959. (Bill Swisher)

CARRIER ALL-WEATHER ATTACK

With the redesignation of July 1956, VC-33 and VC-35 became all-weather attack squadrons VA(AW)-33 and VA(AW)-35 respectively, and on 30 June 1959 VA(AW)-33 was redesignated a carrier airborne early warning squadron VAW-33.

(Below) AD-5N (135020) of VA(AW)-33, DET-42 flying from FORRESTAL (CVA-59) during October of 1958. Their mission of all-weather attack in the jet era is noted by the 'Snoopy' flying dog house on the lower engine cowl. (USN)

CARRIER ALL-WEATHER ATTACK

VA(AW)-33	GD	(Redesignated VAW-33 1959)
VA(AW)-35	VV	(Decom 1959)

(Below) AD-5N (132535) of VA(AW)-35 from ATG-4 after having deployed aboard BENNINGTON (CVA-20) from August of 1958 through January of 1959 to WestPac. ATG-4 was de-established at the close of this cruise. (Bill Swisher)

CARRIER AIRBORNE EARLY WARNING

With the redesignation of Composite Squadrons to Airborne Early Warning Squadrons (VAW) in July of 1956, the newly designated VAW-11 and VAW-12 received the Douglas AD-5W (EA-1E) Skyraider, known as the 'Guppy' because of its pregnant look. The VAW mission was to provide all-weather protection for the Fleet and shore based warning nets. During 1958 the AD-5Q (EA-1F) Skyraider and the Grumman TF-1Q (EC-1A) Tracker were assigned to the squadrons to add ECM capability to their mission. The TF-1Q was based on the Grumman WF-2 (E-1B) Tracker with an enlarged fuselage and additional avionics. The following year, on 30 June 1959, VA(AW)-33 was redesignated as VAW-33 with their mix of aircraft types being reduced to the AD-5Q and the TF-1Q. TF-1Qs were normally used during shore based deployments. On 1 September VAW-13 was established at Agana, Guam and allocated the Grumman WF-2, the AD-5Q and the AD-5W. Their mission was to supply two plane DETs to provide ECM and VAW capability to carriers deploying to the Western Pacific. In 1961 VAW-13 was

transferred to Alameda and their aircraft complement was changed to the AD-5Q for carrier DETs only.

The WF-2 Tracker was first received by VAW-11 of the Pacific Fleet in December 1958. The WF-2 was based on the S2F (S-2) ASW aircraft and mounted a large radar dish atop the fuselage which permitted altitude finding to support control of the Carrier Air Patrol (CAP). VAW-12 of the Atlantic Fleet received the WF-2 the following year, in 1959. The first DET deployed was by VAW-11 in April of 1960 and the last AD-5W DET deployment was in January of 1961. The Tracker provided longer time on station and improved radar. By 1960 the WF-2 had replaced all other aircraft types serving with VAW-11 and VAW-12 in support of the CVA carriers. In 1962 VAW-12 began the anti-submarine (ASW) role with its WF-2s aboard RANDOLPH (CVA-15), with VAW-12 following in 1964. DETs were normally three to four WF-2s. Both squadrons were relocated during this time with VAW-11 going to North Island and VAW-12 to Norfolk. VAW-13 and VAW-33 continued to operate AD-5Ws in support of the CVS carriers.

CARRIER AIRBORN EARLY WARNING

VAW-11	RR	VAW-12	GE	VAW-13	VR	VAW-33	GD

(Above) AD-5Q (132599) of VAW-13 at Point Mugu in May of 1962. They were based at Alameda deploying in three plane DETs for the ECM mission aboard WestPac carriers. (Clay Jansson)

(Above) WF-2 (148141) of VAW-12 preparing for launch from ROOSEVELT (CVA-42) in June of 1960 somewhere in the Med. They returned to CONUS in August. (USN)

(Above) AD-5W (135219) Skyraider 'Guppy' of VAW-12, DET-42 Bats in the Med during October of 1958 providing ASW/AEW for FORRESTAL (CVA-59). (USN)

(Below) EA-1E (AD-5W) (135187) Skyraider of VAW-33, DET-39 after returning from a cruise aboard LAKE CHAMPLAIN (CVS-39) in late 1963. (Roger Besecker)

(Above) AD-5W (135180) of VAW-12 taxiing forward for take-off from ESSEX (CVS-9) in early 1960. Those DETs serving aboard ASW carriers (CVS) carried their own squadron tail codes since CVSGs were not established until mid 1960. (USN)

(Below) WF-2 of VAW-12, DET-42 attached to CVG-8 on FORRESTAL (CVA-59) during 1961. The application of a 400 series nose number resulted when VA-81 did not deploy leaving this series open. (Duane Kasulka Collection)

FIGHTER PHOTOGRAPHIC

Fighter photographic Squadrons employed the Grumman F9F-8P (RF-9P) Cougar and the McDonnell F2H-2P (RF-2B) Banshee, with the primary type being the Cougar. In September of 1957 the first Chance Vought F8U-1P (RF-8A) Crusader was received and quickly began replacing the Cougars and the remaining Banshees. VFP-61 also inventoried the F9F-8B (AF-9J), the F2H-2 (F-2B), and the F9F-6P (RF-9F), but by the summer of 1957 all these aircraft types were gone. In 1957 one DET of VFP-62 sent three F2H-2P Banshees and a single F3D-2T2 (TF-10B) Skyknight aboard FORRESTAL. On 1 July 1959 VFP-63 was redesignated Composite Photographic Squadron 63 (VCP-63) and received the Douglas A3D-2P (RA-3B) Skywarrior, a photographic version of the attack Skywarrior, for long range photographic carrier operations. In 1961 the Navy removed VCP-63's A3D-2Ps and the squadron was designated VFP-63 on 1 July. They also flew a mix of the Lockheed TV-2 and the Beech SNB-5P (RC-45J).

FIGHTER PHOTOGRAPHIC

VFP-61/VCP-63/VFP-63	PP	VFP-62	GA

(Above) F9F-8P (141695) of VFP-61 at Miramar in August of 1957. West Coast DETs in this time period normally maintained the parent squadron's tail code rather than adopt the CVG's tail code. (Bill Larkins)

(Below) F8U-1P (144622) Crusader of VFP-62, DET-42 on FORRESTAL (CVA-59) for her cruise from September 1958 through March 1959 to the Med. Trim colors are Maroon. (USN)

(Left) F8U-1P (144611) of VFP-62 in storage at Litchfield Park in 1960. The squadron markings are typical except for the tail codes, since they deployed carrying both CVG tail codes and their own as well. (Bill Swisher)

(Below) A3D-2P (144847) of VCP-63 at Miramar in May of 1961. The squadron was redesignated VFP-63 in July of 1961 after giving up the A3D when long range reconnaissance was dropped from their mission. (Clay Jansson via Gordon Williams)

(Above) RF-8A (F8U-1P) (146876) of VFP-63, DET-F at Miramar in January of 1963, a month before they deployed with CVG-14 aboard CONSTELLATION (CVA-64). The trim stripe is Blue with White stars. (Clay Jansson)

(Above) RF-8A (F8U-1P) (146889) photo Crusader of VFP-62, DET-59 which returned in March of 1963 from a Med cruise aboard FOR-RESTAL (CVA-59) and was deployed again in 1964 as the same DET. (USN)

(Below) RF-8A (F8U-1P) (146889) of VFP-62, DET-65 during their 1963 cruise aboard ENTERPRISE (CVAN-65) in the Med. A Green Dragon is painted on the nose plus the squadron Pointer dog on the mid fuselage under the wing. (USN)

HEAVY PHOTOGRAPHIC

The mainstay of carrier long range heavy photography was the North American AJ-2P Savage operating from MIDWAY and FORRESTAL class carriers in one or two plane DETs. The new Douglas A3D Skywarrior was modified with twelve cameras for the carrier long range photograhic role under the designation A3D-2P (RA-3B) and began reaching the Fleet during 1959. VAP-61, based at Guam, acquired the additional mission of light photographic reconnaissance in July of 1959, being re-equipped with the Chance Vought F8U-1P (RF-8A) Crusader VCP-61 was redesignated VCP-61. This lasted two years when the squadron reverted back to its original role and designation (VAP-61). Support aircraft operated during this time period included the Beech SNB-5P (RC-45J) and Grumman F9F-8P (RF-9J) Cougar. VAP-62 also operated a Lockheed P2V-3W Neptune which was phased out by mid 1957.

VAP-61/VCP-61/VAP-61	SS	VAP-62	GB

(Below Left) A3D-2P (144834) Skywarrior of VCP-61 based at Guam. VAP-61 had been redesignated to VCP-61 when light photographic reconnaissance was added to their mission in July of 1959. They were redesignated back to VAP-61 two years later. (USN via Bruce Trombecky)

(Below) A3D-2P (144340) of VAP-61 during March of 1961. The photo-reconnaissance Skywarrior had replaced the AJ-2P Savage by 1960. (USN)

HELICOPTER UTILITY

The helicopters in initially service included almost every helicopter type in the Naval inventory. They included the Sikorsky H04S-3, HRS-3, HSS-1, the Bell HTL-3/-4/-5, HUL-1, and the Piasecki HUP-2. HU-1 and HU-2 supplied DETs to both carriers and other types of ships. On 1 July 1960 HU-4 was formed from HU-2 to provide DETs to non aviation ships for the Atlantic Fleet. No similar squadron was created for the Pacific Fleet and HU-1 continued to support both carriers and non aviation ships. Those DETs serving aboard carriers normally deployed with the HO4S, HRS, and HUP with the HO4S being replaced by the HU-2 in 1959. As they became available the Kamen HUK-1 and the Sikorsky HUS-1A were added. The twin engine Beech SNB-5 was used by HU squadrons as a utility aircraft and lasted through 1959. By the end of 1963 helicopter types had been reduced for carrier DETs to only the Kamen HU2K-1 (UH-2A). Other helicopter types and their new designations included the HUL-1 (UH-13P), the HTL-7 (TH-13N), the HSS-1/-1A (UH-34D/-34E), the HU2K-1/-1U (UH-2A/-2B), the HRS-3 (CH-19E), and HUP-2 (UH-25B). A S2F-3 (S-2D) was employed as an utility aircraft by HU-2 during 1963. During 1962 HU-2 operated some A4D-2/-2N (A-4B/C) Skyhawks with a three plane DET at Jacksonville, FL and at Lakehurst, NJ. Carrier DETs were two aircraft, with non aviation DETs being one or two aircraft. HU-4 a non-carrier squadron also operated an F3D-2T2 (EF-10B) Skyknight and three F8U-1P (RF-8A) Crusaders during 1962.

(Above) HUK-1 (146323) of HU-2 delivering a passenger to a destroyer during April of 1960. (USN)

(Left) HUS-1A (145728) of HU-1 at Ream Field in 1962. The HUS-1 carried twelve passengers. Colors are overall International Orange with a Yellow danger band near the tail rotor. (Clay Jansson)

(Below) CH-19E (HRS-3) (137840) of HU-4 at Lakehurst in late 1963. (Clay Jansson)

(Left) UH-2A (HU2K-1) (149774) Seasprite of HU-1 at Ream Field in April of 1963. The UH-2A rapidly became the type assigned to attack carrier groups/wings to perform in the plane guard role. In the plane guard role the helicopter hovered near the carrier during launch and recovery to pick any crewmen that wound up in the drink. (Clay Jansson)

(Below) HRS-3 (130146) of HU-1 at Ream Field in August of 1962. (Clay Jansson)

(Above) HUP-2 (130007) of HU-2 recovering aboard LAKE CHAMPLAIN (CVS-39) in February of 1958. A pair of HSS-1N Seabats of HS-5 have already recovered and sit on the deck. (USN via Fred Roos)

(Below) HSS-1N (145694) Seabat of HU-1 at Ream Field in August of 1962. The Seabat was redesignated SH-34J in the aircraft designation change implemented in September of 1962. (Clay Jansson)

HELICOPTER UTILITY

HU-1	UP	HU-2	HU	HU-4	HT

Attack Carrier Air Groups/Wings and Squadrons/DETs (Dec 1963)

ROOSEVELT· — CVG/CVW-1 AB

Squadron	Aircraft
VF-11	F-8E
VF-14	F-4B
VA-12	A-4C
VA-15	A-1H
VA-172	A-4C
VAH-11	A-3B
●VFP-62	RF-8A
●VAW-12	E-1B
●HU-2	UH-2A

MIDWAY — CVG/CVW-2 NE

Squadron	Aircraft
VF-21	F-4B
VF-24	F-8C
VA-22	A-4C
VA-23	A-4E
VA-25	A-1H/J
VAH-8	A-3B
●VFP-63	RF-8A
●VAW-11	E-1B
●HU-1	UH-2A

SARATOGA· — CVG/CVW-3 AC

Squadron	Aircraft
VF-31	F-3B
VF-32	F-8D
VA-34	A-4C
VA-35	A-1H
VA-36	A-4C
VAH-9	A-3B
●VFP-62	RF-8A
●VAW-12	E-1B
●HU-2	UH-25B
●VQ-2	EA-3B

TICONDEROGA· — CVG/CVW-5 NF

Squadron	Aircraft
VF-51	F-8E
VF-53	F-8E
VA-52	A-1H/J
VA-55	A-4E
VA-56	A-4E
●VAH-4	A-3B
●VFP-63	RF-8A
●VAW-11	E-1B
●HU-1	UH-2A

ENTERPRISE· — CVG/CVW-6 AE

Squadron	Aircraft
VF-33	F-8E
VF-102	F-4B
VA-64	A-4C
VA-65	A-1H
VA-66	A-4C
VA-76	A-4C
VAH-7	A-5A
●VFP-62	RF-8A
●VAW-12	E-1B
●VAW-33	EA-1F
HU-2	UH-2B

INDEPENDENCE — CVG/CVW-7 AG

Squadron	Aircraft
VF-41	F-4B
VF-84	F-8C
VA-72	A-4C
VMA-324	A-4B
VA-86	A-4C
VAH-1	A-5A
●VFP-62	RF-8A
●VAW-12	E-1B
●VAW-33	EA-1F
●HU-2	UH-2A

FORRESTAL· — CVG/CVW-8 AJ

Squadron	Aircraft
VF-74	F-4B
VF-103	F-8C
VA-81	A-4E
VA-83	A-4E
VA-85	A-1E/H
VAH-5	A-3B
●VFP-62	RF-8A
●VAW-12	E-1B
●VAW-33	EA-1F
●HU-2	UH-25C

RANGER — CVG/CVW-9 NG

Squadron	Aircraft
VF-92	F-4B
VF-96	F-4B
VA-93	A-4B/C
VA-94	A-4C
VA-95	A-1H/J
VAH-6	A-3B
●VFP-63	RF-8A
●VAW-11	E-1B
●HU-1	UH-2A

SHANGRI-LA — CVG/CVW-10 AK

Squadron	Aircraft
VF-13	F-3B
VF-62	F-8E
VA-46	A-4C
VA-106	A-4C
VA-176	A-1H
●VAW-12	E-1B
●VFP-62	RF-8A
●VMA-225	A-4C
●HU-2	UH-2B

KITTYHAWK — CVG/CVW-11 NH

Squadron	Aircraft
VF-111	F-8D
VF-114	F-4B
VA-112	A-4C
VA-113	A-4C
VA-115	A-1H
VAH-13	A-3B
●VFP-63	RF-8A
●VAW-11	E-1B
●HU-1	UH-2A

CONSTELLATION — CVG/CVW-14 NK

Squadron	Aircraft
VF-142	F-4B
VF-143	F-4B
VA-144	A-4C
VA-145	A-1H/J
VA-146	A-4C
VAH-10	A-3B
●VFP-63	RF-8A
●VAW-11	E-1B
●HU-1	UH-25B

CORAL SEA — CVG/CVW-15 NL

Squadron	Aircraft
VF-151	F-3B
VF-154	F-8D
VA-152	A-1H/J
VA-153	A-4C
VA-155	A-4B/E
VAH-2	A-3B
●VFP-63	RF-8A
●VAW-11	E-1B
●HU-1	UH-25B

ORISKANY — CVG/CVW-16 AH

Squadron	Aircraft
VF-161	F3B
VF-162	F-8A
VA-163	A-4B
VA-164	A-4B ●
VA-165	A-1H/J
●VAH-4	A-3B
●VFP-63	RF-8A
●VAW-11	E-1B
●HU-1	UH-2A

BON HOMME RICHARD — CVG/CVW-19 NM

Squadron	Aircraft
VF-191	F-8E
VF-194	F-8C
VA-192	A-4C
VA-195	A-4C
VA-196	A-1H/J
●VAH-4	A-3B
●VFP-63	RF-8A
●VAW-11	E-1B
●HU-1	UH-2A

HANCOCK — CVG/CVW-21 NF

Squadron	Aircraft
VF-211	F-8A
VF-213	F-3B
VA-212	A-4B
VA-215	A-1H
VA-216	A-4C
●VAH-4	A-3B
●VFP-63	RF-8A
●VAW-11	E-1B
●HU-1	UH-25B

● *Deployed as DETs*
* *Carriers and CVG/CVW stateside.*

During 1963 all attack carrier air groups (CVG/RCVG) were redesignated as attack carrier air wings (CVW/RCVW). There was no change with the ASW air groups. When the new tail codes for air groups were assigned in late 1956 those tail codes beginning with 'N' were Pacific Fleet, and those beginning with the letter 'A' were Atlantic Fleet.

REPLACEMENT ATTACK CARRIER SQUADRONS

Squadrons that initially made up the two new RCVGs in 1958 were mainly Fleet squadrons with a change in mission. In addition to those aircraft assigned for FIP and crew training were an assortment of specialty and utility aircraft. RCVG-4 of the Atlantic Fleet was assigned VF-21, VF-101, VF-174, VA-42, and VA-44. VF-21 retained their F11F-1 (F-11A) Tigers and added the F9F-8T (TF-9J) Cougars, T-33Bs, and T-28B Trojans. In November F11F Tigers were replaced by the A4D (A-4) Skyhawk. VF-101 was assigned training of the F4D-1 (F-6A) Skyray and F3H (F-3) Demon, with the F3D-2T2 (TF-10B) Skyknight, T-33B, and R4D-5 (C-47H) for support aircraft. VF-174 retained its F8U (F-8) Crusaders and VA-42 its AD (A-1) Skyraiders. VA-44 had A4Ds and added the F9F-8T (TF-9J), T-33B, and T-28B. In February of 1959 VA-44 acquired the A4D Skyhawk when VA-105 was disestablished. In July VF-21 was redesignated VA-43 when they switched to A4D Skyhawk training.

RCVG-12 of the Pacific Fleet had VF-121, VF-124, VA-122, VA-125, and VA-126. VF-121 initially an F3H Demon squadron added the F11F-1 (F-11A) Tiger, FJ Fury, F3D-2T2, T-33B, F9F-8T and T-28. VA-122 retained its AD-6/-7 (A-1H/J) Skyraiders for day attack and added the AD-5 (A-1E) and AD-5N (A-1G) Skyraiders of VA(AW)-35 for all-weather training. VA-125 retained its A4Ds while VA-126 retained its FJ-4 (F-1E) Furies and added a few ADs. Heavy Attack Training Units (HATU) were already in place on each coast as part of Heavy Attack Wing One (Atlantic) at Sanford, and Heavy Attack Wing Two (Pacific) at Whidbey Island. HATULANT was merged into VAH-3 and continued A3D (A-3) Skywarrior training for the Atlantic Fleet. HATUPAC was retained for A3D training on the west coast, and in June of 1959 was redesignated VAH-123 as part of RCVG-12.

In June of 1961 VAH-3 received the first A3J-1 (A-5A) Vigilante to begin its FIP. The following year they received the first of six A3D-2T (TA-3B) Skywarriors which were specifically designed as an airborne bombardier/navigation trainer replacing the previous training aircraft (P2V-3B Neptunes). VAH-3 received the first A3J-3 (RA-5C) during December of 1963, which combined the attack capability of the A-5A with electronic and photographic capability. They also operated a YA-5C for transition training to the RA-5C beginning in mid 1963.

The F4H-1F Phantom II began arriving at VF-121, the Pacific Fleet RAG, and VF-101, the Atlantic Fleet RAG, during December of 1961, beginning the FIP to replace the F3H (F-3) Demon. Another new type, the Grumman A2F-1 (A-6A) Intruder, designed for both limited and nuclear warfare was first introduced in February of 1962 by the Green Pawns of VA-42.

On 15 June 1962 VA-127 was established by redesignating DET-ALPHA from VA-126. Their primary mission was all-weather jet instrument training with the F9F-8T (TF-9J), the two place trainer Cougar. The following year on 15 February VA-45 was reestablished and took over AD (A-1) Skyraider training from VA-44 which was to specialize in (A-4) Skyhawk training.

(Above) F4D-1 (1394917) Skyray of VF-101 Grim Reapers at Sanford in March of 1958. (Bill Swisher)

(Below) F3D-2T2 (125829) Skyknight of VF-101 now in storage at Litchfield Park in March of 1960. The F3D was used for radar officer training and was phased out by VF-101 in late 1959. (Bill Swisher)

(Above) FJ-4B Furys of VA-126 Trailblazers the newly established replacement squadron for instrument training for RCVG-12. VA-126 was originally commissioned in April of 1956 as a Fleet tactical squadron and equipped with F7U Cutlasses. (USN)

(Below) F3H-2 (137030) Demon of VF-121 at Litchfield Park in 1963 awaiting storage. Sufficient pilots existed within the Fleet to support those Demon squadrons still operational. (Bill Swisher)

(Left) F9F-8T (142467) Cougar VF-21 used to support F11F training was redesignated VA-43 when they changed from F11F Tiger training to A4D Skyhawk training in July of 1959. (USN via Jim Sullivan)

(Below Left) AD-7 (142029) Skyraider of VA-122 trimmed in International Orange and was the only squadron in RCVG-12 used for Skyraider training. Moffett Field in May of 1962. (Bill Larkins)

(Below) F11F-1 (141808) of VF-21 at Wilmington, NC in April of 1961. The training role of the Tiger ended at this time since the Fleet squadrons were turning their Tigers in. (Jim Sullivan)

(Above) A4D-2 (144935) Skyhawk of VA-43 recovering aboard AN-TIETAM (CVS-36) during 1960. The Skyhawk squadrons of RCVG-4 during this time period applied their aircraft number on the fuselage behind the intake. (USN)

(Above) F8U-1 (145400) of VF-124 aboard LEXINGTON (CVA-16) in August of 1961. The use of Gull Gray over Insignia White with International Orange trim was typical of aircraft within RCVG-4 and RCVG-12. (Larry Kasulka)

(Above) SAGEBURNER, an F4H-1F (143307) Phantom II flown by Lt H Hardisty and Lt E DeEsch of VF-101 Grim Reapers, DET-Alpha from Oceana established a new speed record of 902.8 MPH over a three kilometer course at Holloman AFB on 28 August 1961. The special project trim band is the International Orange used for high visibility. (USN)

(Above) A3D-1s of VAH-123 at North Island in March of 1961. High visibility International Orange Red over Gloss White was used by those aircraft dedicated to a training role. (USN)

(Below) A-6A (A2F-1) Intruder of VA-42 replaced their prior training aircraft, the Skyraider, in February of 1962 at Oceana. The first Fleet Intruder squadron, VA-75, began conversion to the A-6 in September of 1963. (USN)

(Above) YA-5C (YA3J-3) (149305) Vigilante was one of five interim training aircraft used by VAH-3 for transitioning from the A-5A to the RA-5C. The first YA-5C was received in June of 1963. (Al Bachmann)

CARRIER TRAINING UNITS (DECEMBER 1963)

RCVG/RCVW-4	AD	RCVG-RCVW-12	NJ
VF-101	F-4A/B, TF-9J	VF-121	F-4A/B, F-3B, TF-10B
VF-174	F-8B/C/D/E	VF-124	F-8A/C/D/E
VA-42	A-6A, A-1E, T-28B	VA-122	A-1E, H/J, T-28B
VA-43	A-4C/E, TF-9J, RF-9J	VA-125	A-4B/C/E, A-1E
VA-44	A-4B/C, TF-9J	VA-126	TF-9J
VA-45	A-1E/H, T-28B	VA-127	TF-9J
VAH-3*	TA-3B, A-3A/B, TF-9J, TC-47K, A-5A, RA-5C	VAH-123	A-3A/B, TA-3B

*Used tail code of GJ as originally assigned in November 1956.

ASW CARRIER SQUADRONS

The formerly independent carrier-based VS and HS squadrons were to be formed into ASW air groups (CVSG) with two VS squadrons of twelve aircraft each, one HS squadron of sixteen helicopters, and a VAW DET. Periodically a DET of fighter aircraft was attached to an ASW carrier to provide combat air patrol (CAP) for the defenseless VS and HS squadrons. These fighter DETs normally consisted of four F2H Banshees, but with the phasing out of the Banshee the Navy began using the A4D Skyhawk as a replacement.

CARRIER ANTI-SUBMARINE

BY 1957 the Grumman S2F-1 (S-2A) Tracker, first introduced in 1954, had replaced all Grumman AF Guardians with VS-37 being the last to re-equip in early 1957. CVS carriers initially operated squadrons of twenty S-2s along with a helicopter anti-submarine squadron (HS). With the establishment of formal carrier ASW air groups in 1960 the number of VS squadrons was expanded but at the same time the number of aircraft in each VS squadron was reduced from twenty to twelve.

The S2F-1 with updated avionics was redesignated S2F-1S (S-2B). The S2F-2 (S-2C) followed carrying an enlarged tail section and an enlarged weapons bay capable of carrying a nuclear depth charge or two torpedoes. With final withdrawal of the escort carrier (CVE) from the fleet in late 1957 weight restrictions on the S2F Tracker were relaxed, resulting in the S2F-3 (S-2D). The S2F-3 was a second generation Tracker carrying more fuel, larger wings, larger engine nacelles, and with the capability of carrying sixteen instead of eight sonobuoys. The S2F-3 entered the Fleet in May of 1961. Next followed the S2F-3S (S-2E) which carried new sonobuoys that required a data relay back to the carrier for data processing. The S2F-3S with its upgraded electronics reached the Fleet in August of 1962. Updating the S2F-1S avionics produced the S2F-1S1 (S-2F). The S2F-3 and 3S Trackers could carry four torpedoes under the wings.

During the Berlin confrontation in 1962 the thirteen Reserve ASW squadrons, activated in October, flew S2F-1 (S-2A) Trackers. Several of these squadrons were assigned tail codes previously used by Fleet VS squadrons which had since switched to the use of CVSG tail codes assigned in 1960. VS-872 operated four P2V-5Fs in addition to its ten Trackers for a brief period in 1962.

(Above) SNB-5 (51194) of HS-2 at Ream Field in 1960. HS-2 operated the last SNB used by the HS community as a utility aircraft. Color scheme was the 'split' scheme with Insignia White and International Orange. (Clay Jansson)

(Below) S2F-1 (133382) of VS-21 operating off PHILIPPINE SEA (CVS-47) with their own individual tail codes during 1959. The individual squadron tail codes were replaced by establishing CVSG tail codes during 1960. The implementation of these new codes was similar to that established for the CVGs during the late 1940s. (USN via Bruce Trombecky)

(Above) S2F-1 (136432) of VS-23 Black Cats carrying Red trim and squadron tail code of 'PF' at Salinas, CA in September of 1957. The Black Cats were the first Pacific Fleet squadron to deploy with the Tracker. (Larry Smalley)

(Below) S2F-1 (136707) of VS-28 Hukkers flying from WASP (CVS-18) in February of 1962 as part of Task Group BRAVO. (USN via Fred Roos)

(Above) S2F-3 (136659) of VS-37 at Moffett Field in July of 1959. The rays surrounding the CVSG tail code are Black. (Larry Smalley)

(Above) S2F-1 (136479) of VS-861 was activated at Norfolk during the Berlin Wall crisis of 1962. Some of the activated squadrons adopted very colorful trim markings. Guantanamo Bay, Cuba in January of 1962. (USN via Naval Aviation News)

(Below) S2F-1 (133310) of VS-891, activated from Washington and just visible are the station codes of '7T' is a carry over from the aircraft's previous assignment while based at Seattle. (Clay Jansson)

(Above) S2F-3S (136439) of VS-39 carrying squadron tail codes. The lightning bolt on the aft fuselage beneath the tail plane is Red which was used by most VS squadrons prior to the formal establishment of standard trim colors in 1960. (Frank Hartman)

ANTI-SUBMARINE WARFARE SQUADRONS

Active Fleet					
VS-20	**	VS-28	**	VS-36	ME
VS-21	YA	VS-29	**	VS-37	SU
VS-22	**	VS-30	MB	VS-38	ST
VS-23	PF	VS-31	MC	VS-39	MF
VS-24	**	VS-32	MD	VS-41	**
VS-25	**	VS-33	**	VS-42	**
VS-26	**	VS-34	**	— —	— —
VS-27	MA	VS-35	**	— —	— —

Berlin Reserve Callup					
VS-721	SY	VS-772	SU	VS-873	SV
VS-733	CT	VS-821	CU	VS-891	SX
VS-751	CC	VS-837	CR	VS-915	CS
VS-771	ST	VS-861	CV	VS-935	SP
— —	—	VS-872	SW	—	—

Individual squadron tail codes dropped after mid 1960 when CVSG/RCVSG codes were adopted.
***Squadrons added after CVSG/RCVSG codes were adopted.*

(Below) S2F-1 (133206) of VS-872 at Alameda in July of 1962. The application of a three digit squadron aircraft number was used by some Reserves at their home Air Stations. (Doug Olson via Clay Jansson)

(Below) S2F-2 (133358) of VS-34 in storage at Litchfield Park in March of 1963. The trim colors are Yellow outlined in Black. This aircraft's last cruise was aboard ESSEX (CVS-9) which can be seen on the vertical fin cap. (Doug Olson via Clay Jansson)

HELICOPTER ANTI-SUBMARINE

The Sikorsky HSS-1 (SH-34G) Seahorse, the first true ASW helicopter with a sonar transducer capable of being lowered into the water while the helicopter hovered a few feet above the water. It also carried two homing torpedoes. The HSS-1 had begun to join the Fleet in late 1956 and equipped all squadrons except for two squadrons that operated the Sikorsky HO4S-3 and these were phased out by late 1957. Other types of helicopters in service included the Bell HTL-4 and HTL-5 used by several squadrons that had been established in mid 1956, but had not completed their transition training. In addition each squadron also operated a Beech SNB-5 for utility duties. The HS-2 was phased out with the last one leaving the HS community in 1960.

The HSS-1N (SH-34J) began to arrive in October of 1958, with HS-1 of the Atlantic Fleet and HS-6 of the Pacific Fleet being the first units to receive them. The HSS-1N introduced day and night instrument flying and automatic hovering. The last of the HSS-1s were phased out in 1963 by HS-4 and the HSS-1Ns by HS-5.

Next to enter service was the Sikorsky HSS-2 (SH-3A) Sea King which was the Navy's first jet powered helicopter. It had provisions for increased ordinances, and improved avionics permitting the SH-3A to be an *all-weather* ASW helicopter. Other features included the capability for automatic hovering and emergency water landings. The first Sea Kings arrived in early 1962 and by the end of 1963 all HS squadrons were equipped with them. Normally sixteen helicopters were assigned to each squadron.

With the establishment of ASW Air Groups in 1960 the dedicated tail codes were dropped and squadrons adopted the CVSG/RCVSG tail codes of their assigned air group. At the close of 1963 the ASW helicopter Squadrons were organized into nine Fleet and two training groups.

(Above) HSS-1 (141586) of HS-4 delivering an officer to the ballistic missile submarine ETHAN ALLEN (SSBN-608) in May of 1962. (USN)

(Left) HSS-1N (143883) of HS-2 carrying squadron tail code of 'SN' flying from TICONDEROGA (CVS-14) in 1961. The HS-2 was the first West Coast HS squadron established with their first deployment being in 1957 aboard PHILIPPINE SEA (CVA-47). (USN via Naval Aviation News)

(Below) HSS-1s of HS-6 hovering in the Gull Gray and White initially used by carrier deployed squadrons until 1961 when Engine Gray was adopted for ASW helicopters. The individual squadron tail code was dropped after 1960 when CVSGs were established. (USN via Naval Aviation News)

(Left) HSS-1 (143897) Seahorse of HS-9 carrying a MK-43 torpedo in the firing position near Quonset Point in February of 1959. (USN)

(Below) SH-34J (HSS-1N) (147995) of HS-5 carrying Light Blue and White checkered trim on the tail. Lake Champlain (CVS-39) in February of 1962. (USN)

"

(Above) HUS-1 (143892) of HS-9 Sea Griffens having returned from a cruise aboard ESSEX (CVS-9) in 1962. (Duane Kasulka Collection)

(Right) SH-3A (HSS-2) (149725) of HS-11 deployed aboard WASP (CVS-18) and later temporarily shore based at Roosevelt Road, PR in March of 1963. (USN)

HELICOPTER ANTI-SUBMARINE

HS-1	HA	HS-4	TA	HS-7	HD	HS-10	**
HS-2	SK	HS-5	HC	HS-8	VB	HS-11	HF
HS-3	HB	HS-6	UB	HS-9	HE	HS-13	**

***Squadron added after CVSG/RCVSG Tail Codes were assigned.*

Anti-Submarine Warefare Air Groups with Squadrons and DETs (Dec 1963)

LAKE CHAMPLAIN		KEARSARGE		x WASP		x YORKTOWN		INTREPID		HORNET	
CVSG-52	**AS**	**CVSG-53**	**NS**	**CVSG-54**	**AT**	**CVSG-55**	**NU**	**CVSG-56**	**AU**	**CVSG-57**	**NV**
VS-28	S-2E	VS-21	S-2B/F	VS-22	S-2F	VS-23	S-2E/F	VS-24	S-2F	VS-35	S-2D
VS-31	SH-3A	VS-29	S-2B/F	VS-32	S-2F	VS-25	S-2D/F	VS-27	S-2F	VS-37	S-2D
HS-11	SH-3A	HS-6	SH-3A	HS-5	SH-3A	HS-4	SH-3A/J	HS-3	SH-3A	HS-2	SH-3A
●VAW-3	EA-1E	●VA-22	A-4B	●VAW-33	EA-1E	●VAW-11	EA-1E	●VAW-33	EA-1E	●VMA-214	A-4B
●VA-83	A-4B	●VAW-11	EA-1E							●VAW-11	EA-1E
		●HU-1	UH-2A							●HU-1	UH-2A

RANDOLPH		x BENNINGTON		x ESSEX		RESERVE	
CVSG-58	**AV**	**CVSG-59**	**NT**	**CVSG-60**	**AW**	**CVSG-62**	**AX***
VS-26	S-2D	VS-33	S-2E	VS-34	S-2D	VS-20	S-2F
VS-36	S-2D	VS-38	S-2E	VS-39	S-2D	VS-42	S-2B
HS-7	SH-3A	HS-8	SH-3A	HS-9	SH-3A	HS-13	SH-34J
●VAW-12	E-1B	●VA-93	A-4B	●VAW-33	VA-1E		
		●VAW-11	EA-1E	●VAW-12	E-1B		
		●HU-1	UH-2A				

**Air Group and Sqds commissioned 25 August 1961, de-commissioned 1 October 1962.*
xCarriers and CVSG Stateside
● Depolyed as DETs.

ASW TRAINING UNITS (DECEMBER 1963)

RCVSG-50	AR	RCVSG-51	RA
VS-30	S-2D/E/F	VS-41	S-2A/D/E/F
HS-1	SH-3A	HS-10	SH-3A

REPLACEMENT ANTI-SUBMARINE CARRIER SQUADRONS

Squadrons assigned to the Atlantic Fleet's new RCVSG were Fleet squadrons while those assigned to the Pacific Fleet were newly established. The two replacement CVSGs were established on 30 June 1960 as RCVSG-50 for the Pacific Fleet and RCVSG-51 for the Atlantic Fleet. Each VS squadron was equipped with a variety of S2F (S-2) Trackers and the HS squadrons were equipped with the HSS-1 (SH-34) Seahorse. The first Sikorsky HSS-2 (SH-3A) Sea King arrived in 1961 with HS-1 providing the FIP for the Pacific Fleet RAG HS-10 and the first Fleet squadron HS-3 of CVSG-56.

(Below Left) S-2F (S2F-3) (134738) of VS-30 on a training flight off the coast of the Florida Keys. (Grumman Corp)

(Below) HSS-1 (143925) of HS-1 Seahorse with its sonar loward during a training session off the coast of Florida during June of 1963. The Seahorse was the first all weather helicopter squadron when they transitioned to the HSS-1N in October of 1958.

ELECTRONIC COUNTER-MEASURE/FLEET AIR RECONNAISSANCE

Fleet electronic countermeasure Squadron (VQ) had its beginnings in 1951 as a special project and during 1953 the function was given to VAW-1 as DET ALPHA in the Pacific Fleet. DET ALPHA was reorganized in June of 1955 and designated VQ-1. VQ-2 was established during September for the Atlantic Fleet at Fort Lyauty, Morocco, but later moved to Rota, Spain. During this time period VQ-1 was based at Atsugi, Japan. Initially equipped with landbased Lockheed P2V Neptunes and Martin P4M-1Q Mercators. They began supplying DETs to carriers with the arrival of the A3D-2Q (EA-3B) in 1959. The Lockheed WV-2Q (EC-121M) Warning Star was added in 1960 to replace the P2V and P4M for long range landbased patrols. VQ-1 also operated several A3Ds. On 1 January 1960 these two squadrons were redesignated Fleet Air Reconnaissance without a letter change.

(Above) EA-3B (A3D-2Q) Skywarrior of VQ-2 were specially built with a pressurized cabin housing four ECM operators in place of the bomb bay. In addition to the extra ECM gear side and forward looking radar and infra-red sensors were also carried. Twenty five were built. (MDAC via HARRY GANN)

GUIDED MISSILE UNITS

A variety of guided missile squadrons/groups were established with the advent of the guided missile in the 1950s and several supplied DETs for carrier deployments. Of those that supported carrier operations there was Guided Missile Group One and Two (GMGRU-1 and 2) established on 16 September and 26 September 1956 respectively. GMGRU-1 was based at North Island but later moved to Barbers Point while GMGRU-2 was established at Chincoteague, VA later moving to Port Lyautey. GMGRU-2 was disestablished in January of 1958, being replaced by Guided Missile Support Squadron Two (GMSRon-2) which in turn was redesignated Utility Squadron eight (VU-8) in 1960. GMGRU-1 and -2 were normally landbased commands operating a few aircraft from carriers as missile controllers for the Chance Vought Regulas Surface-to-Surface missile. These DETs were equipped with one or two FJ-3D (DF-1C) Fury. They operatedthese DETs till disestablished in 1960. Aircraft used for shore duties included the F9F-5KD (DF-9E) Panther, F9F-6D (DF-9F) Cougar, TV-2D (DT-33B), FJ-4 (F-1E), and FJ-3D2 (DF-1D).

AIR DEVELOPMENT

One other land based squadron was known to have operated a DET aboard a carrier. Air Development Squadron Four (VX-4) operated three F7U-3M Cutlasses from SHANGRI LA from November of 1956 thru May of 1957 attached to CVG-2 as DET-A.

ELECTRONIC COUNTERMEASURE

VQ-1	PR		VQ-2	JG

(Above) P4M-1Q Mercators of VQ-1 were initially used in the ECM role assigned to land based squadrons but were quickly replaced with the arrival of the carrier capable A3D-2Q Skywarrior in 1960. (Clay Jansson)

GUIDED MISSILES GROUPS

GMGRU-1	ZZ	(Decom 1960)
GMGRU-2/GMSRon-2	GF	(Redesignated VU-8)

(Above) FJ-3D (136018) of GMGRU-1 used their Fury's as missile controllers from 1956 through 1960 when they were disestablished. This Fury is in storage at Litchfield in March of 1960. (Bill Swisher)

(Below) F7U-3M (139703) Cutlass of VX-4 now a non-flight aircraft used for O&R training. The markings are those used during its CVG-2 cruise aboard SHANGRI LA (CVA-38) in 1956/57, which deployed as DET-A with three Cutlasses. Trim colors are Dark Blue outlined in Red with White stars. (Bill Swisher)